GARY JONES

Greece

First edition

This book was professionally typeset on Reedsy.
Find out more at reedsy.com

Contents

1

ATHENS INTRODUCTION

I want to thank you and congratulate you for downloading the book, "Athens Travel Guide: How to Enjoy Your 3 Day Athens Vacation".

Athens is one of the oldest cities in the world. It was once the home of the ancient Gods and Goddesses. It is the birthplace of Western civilization and democracy. It's a land of ancient temples, theatres, and even the Olympic Games. It is a historical and cultural melting pot.

This city is a combination of old and new. It has captivating ancient temples and a fair share of urban monoliths. You could climb up to the Acropolis to see the breathtaking panoramic view of the city. It was also once the home of the most brilliant minds in the world.

Athens is definitely a memorable travel destination that you should visit at least once in your lifetime.

This book is your ultimate travel guide to the ancient city of Athens. In this book, you'll find all the information you'll need to organize a 3 days Athens trip, including:

- Athens' rich and fascinating history
- What's the best time to go
- How to get around the city
- The most interesting and stunning cafes in the cities
- The most thought-provoking and visually stimulating museums
- The most famous landmarks in the city
- Where to eat
- The best budget friendly hotels
- Things that you can only do in Athens
- The best night bars and clubs
- Travel and safety tips
- Insider tips that will help you get the most out of your trip
- And more!

This book has everything you need to keep your trip fun, interesting, and hassle free. Athens is one gem of a city. It's filled with stunning historical sites that would definitely leave a mark in your memory. This book will give you all the information you need, so you would not miss everything that this wonderful and unforgettable city has to offer.

Thank you again for downloading this book and I hope that you enjoy it!

2

Athens: The Birthplace of Democracy and Western Civilization

Athens is one of the most marvelous cities that you'll ever visit in your lifetime. It is the birthplace of the democracy and Western civilization.

We wouldn't be able to enjoy the opportunity to choose our own leaders if it's not for the great minds of the Athenians. It is also the center of philosophy, cartography, geometry, and the Olympic. There's something about this lovely city that puts you in a meditative state. It is an intellectual center as much as it is a cultural hot spot. It was the home of some of the greatest minds of the history of mankind, including Socrates, Plato, and Solon. It was also once the home of the greatest philosopher of the ancient times – Aristotle.

Athens is one of the most scenic cities in the world. At its center lies the great Acropolis, the great ancient city which was once the political and religious center of Greece.

Today, Athens is the home of countless museums, universities, shopping malls, government buildings, and interesting neighborhoods. It's a place where the old meets the new. It's truly a wonderful and glorious place. No adjective is enough to describe its mystery, beauty, and glory.

The Rich History of Athens

Athens was thousands of years ahead of its time. It was the center of creativity, power, and ambition. It is a city of intellects, philosophers, and geniuses. It was often called the Ancient Silicon Valley.

The "city of the violet crown" got its name from its patron goddess – Athena. According to the legends and myths found in the works of Ovid, Herodotus, and Plutarch, both Poseidon (the god of the sea) and Athena (the goddess of wisdom) wanted to be the patron of the city. And so, a contest was held to determine which god is worthy of becoming the city's patron.

Poseidon made a spring in the middle of the city. This symbolizes naval power. Athena, on the other hand, created an olive tree which symbolizes wealth and peace. Cecrops, the mythical king of the city, accepted Athena's gift and named the city after her. It was said that the tree was located at the top of the Acropolis.

According to historians, a number of people lived in the city during the New Stone Age at the end of 4th millennium BC. By 1412 BC, Athens has become the center of the Mycenaean Civilization or the "bronze age". By this time, the Athenians built a Mycenaean fortress on the Acropolis. This is the foundation of Western Civilization. This fortress has Cyclopean walls and you could still a part of these walls today.

Athens was formerly ruled by Kings, including Cecrops I, Erichthonius, Pandion I, Theseus, and Apheidas. These kings were the leaders of the land-owning aristocracy called "Eupatridae", meaning well-born. For years, the rich families ruled in Athens. During this time, there was an ongoing conflict between the poor and the rich. To resolve this conflict, an aristocrat named Solon created a set of rules called the Solonian Law. He removed the privileges of the rich families and divided the Athenians into four classes. Each class has a separate governing body. Each class can elect officials. Solon created a set of rules called the Solonian Law. This law allowed more people to participate in the government. This is the start of what is now known as "democracy".

The 5th century BC is considered the "golden age" of the city. It was the time when the Parthenon was built. The Athenian art and philosophy were thriving during this time. But, the golden age ended when a war erupted between the Sparta and the Athenians.

By the 2nd century BC, Greece was under the power of the Roman Empire. The Romans ruled Greece for 500 years, but even during this time, Athens continued to be the home of philosophers, mathematicians, and intellectuals.

Athens was under the Byzantine rule in 529 AD. Constantine I founded the Byzantine Empiere and it's based in a city called Constantinople (now known as Istanbul). Byzantine art is mainly focused on religion. These artworks are colorful and have a mosaic-like texture. This was a great and prosperous period.

In 1204, the Latins conquered Athens and ruled until 1458, when it officially became a part of the Ottoman Empire.

The Greek revolution erupted in 1821 and Greece became an independent country in 1830. A Bavarian prince named Otto became the King of Greece. During this time, the residents of Athens lived in a quaint neighborhood named Plaka.

For a while Athens was a peaceful city until it fell in the hands of the Nazis during the World War II. It was a dark time for the city. But, after the war, Athens began to grow as many people around Europe and Asia migrated to the city, looking for better opportunities. Greece experienced a huge debt crisis in 2010. This led to unemployment and reduced pensions.

However, even if Athens went through an economic crisis, it remained as one of the most beautiful cities in the world.

3

Things You Need to Know Before Visiting Athens

Athens is a picture-perfect city with beautiful sights, marble temples, palace-like government buildings, fascinating museums, quirky restaurants, and even street art.

If you're traveling to Athens for the first time, below are a few things that you need to know.

The Athens Weather

Like most European cities, Athens has all the four seasons. It doesn't get too hot during the summer. It almost feels like you're in a tropical country. The Acropolis looks golden under the summer sun. It's also the best time to go to the beach and just enjoy the beauty of the flowers and the warmth of the turquoise sea.

If you're traveling to Athens during the summer months, make sure to bring an umbrella or a hat. It is the perfect time to take a day trip to fabulous Greek Islands such as Aegina, Hydra, and Spetses.

Athens is blooming in spring time. The weather is temperate – not too cold, not too hot. It's the perfect time to walk around the city and just enjoy the panoramic Athenian view. Tourist spots can get a little crowded during this time, though.

Athens looks stunning during the autumn season. The Acropolis is perched above a sea of beautiful building and red, purple, yellow, brown, and pink trees. The weather is cooler in October. Some autumn days are so warm that you'll think it's still summer time.

The winter in Athens is not at all brutal. The temperatures are usually range from 7 degrees Celsius to 18 degrees Celsius. The Acropolis almost looks like a ghost town during winter time. Hence, if you want to avoid the tourist groups and get good hotel rates, you should visit Athens in the winter.

Below are Athens' average temperatures by month:

Month Average Temperature in Celsius

December 11 degrees

November 14 degrees

October 18 degrees

September 24 degrees

August 28 degrees

July 29 degrees

June 20 degrees

May 19 degrees

April 16 degrees

March 12 degrees

February 10 degrees

January 9 degrees

Best Time To Visit Athens

Athens is most beautiful during the summer time. But, during this time, temperatures can go up to 33 degrees Celsius. Days can get too hot. This is also the city's tourism peak, so the hotel rates are expensive, and the tourist spots are filled with tourists. This is the reason why the best time to visit Athens is between March and May (Spring) and between September to November (Autumn).

4

Transport And Safety

Athens has a well-developed transport system, making it easier to go around. There are a number of ways to get around the city – rental cars, the metro, buses, trolleys, trams, and taxis.

Metro

The best way to explore Athens is through the subway/metro. The Athens metro has three lines, namely:

- 1 The Green Line (route: Piraeus to Kifisia; passes through 24 stations)

- 2 The Red Line (route: Anthoupoli to Elliniko; passes through 20 stations, this takes you to the touristy areas)
- 3 The Blue Line (route: Agia Marina to Doukissis Palakentias; passes through 20 stations)

These trains connect the most popular landmarks in Athens. You could find train stations in "touristy" neighborhoods.

Buses and Trolleys (Electric Buses)

Buses and trolleys are popular in Athens. More than 300 bus lines operate from 6am to 11pm in the city. But, buses traveling from the Athens Airport to the Port of Piraeus and Syntagma usually operate 24 hours. The regular buses are usually blue, and the trolleys are yellow.

Tram

Athens has a tram network system that has three lines and 48 stops.
There are three tram lines and routes, namely:

- 1. Blue (route: Faliro Metro Station to Asklippio Voulas; passes through 31 stops)
- 2. Red (route: Faliro Metro Station to Syntagma; passes through 28 stops)
- 3. Green (route: Syntagma to Asklippio Voulas; passes through 37)

Taxi

You can easily find taxis everywhere in the city. A regular 3-kilometer ride usually costs 5.72 euros.

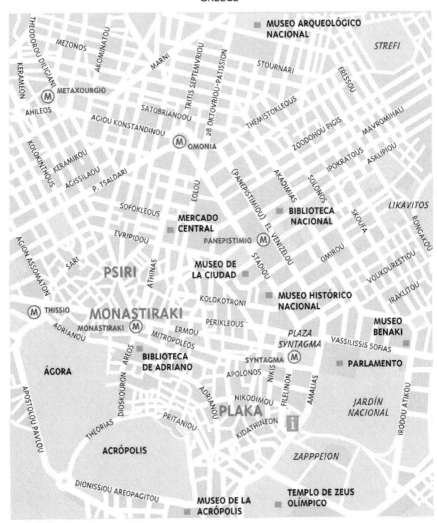

Athens Map

Safety and Travel Tips

Athens is generally safe. It's even great for lone female backpackers. But, like many metropolitan cities, some areas in Athens are filled with pickpockets and thieves.

Athens is a popular tourist spot, so it's no surprise that you could find a lot of pickpockets in the city. There are con artists preying on tourists in the city's major landmarks, especially the Acropolis. Beware of people offering to carry your luggage, some of these people may be thieves.

Keep an eye on your personal belongings, especially if you are on a bus or a train. Also, there are a lot of taxi scams around the city. There are cab drivers who set higher rates for foreigners. Some taxi drivers also pretend to forget to turn on the meter, so they can charge more than they should. There are also a lot of scammers in bars and club, so be careful. It is hard to spot scammers because some are well-dressed and well-mannered.

Here's a list of travel tips that can help make your Athens vacation more fun and hassle-free:

1.If you're on a tight budget, stay in hostels. This is also a good place to meet new friends.

2.Meals in touristy Plaka could cost around 40 euros. But, cafés usually charge around 12 euros. If you're on a budget, try street food. A lot of street vendors sell pizzas and gyros (Greek shawarma) for only 4 euros.

3.Dine at Plaka at least once. It's an expensive place but the food is worth the price.

4.Cash is king in Greece. When you're traveling to Athens, make sure that you have enough Euros. A few stores take cards.

5.Athens is a smoking city, so expect to see smokers everywhere.

6.Nightlife in Athens starts late. A lot of locals go out at 1 am or 2 am.

7.Most restaurants collect service fees, so you don't have to give tips.

8.Learn some commonly used Greek words:

- Good morning – Kalimera
- Good night – Kalinitha
- Good evening – Kalispera
- Thank you – Efharisto
- Hello – Ya or yassas
- Please – Parakalo
- Excuse me – Signomi
- Do you speak English – Milatay Agglika?
- I don't speak Greek – The milao ellinika.

9.Greeks usually close their stores at noon for their siesta break. So, if you need to buy something, do it in the morning.

10.Most tourist attractions are within walking distance from each other. You can save money when you walk from one place to another. Wear something comfortable when you around the Acropolis and Plaka. Most streets are elevated and located on the slopes of a mountain.

Finally, just enjoy the experience. Take as much photos as you can and live in the moment. You are, after all, in one of the most interesting and enchanting cities in the world.

5

The Best Tourist Spots in Athens

Acropolis

Athens has a rich (and almost mythical) history. It is the land of gods and goddesses. It was once the home of the wisest philosophers in the history. This modern city looks like a sea of skyscrapers and urban monoliths. But, some parts of the city gives you a glimpse of what

Ancient Greece is like and why it was way ahead of its time.

The Acropolis and its Three Grand Structures – the Parthenon, the Propylaea, and the Erechtheion

The Acropolis is in every traveler's bucket list. This ancient city is nestled on a massive rock overlooking the quaint neighborhoods of Athens. The Acropolis is the foundation of Western Civilization. It's a complex of temples dedicated to their gods. It is the highest point of the city, about 150 meters above ground.

The Acropolis is the crowning glory of Athens and its most important landmark.

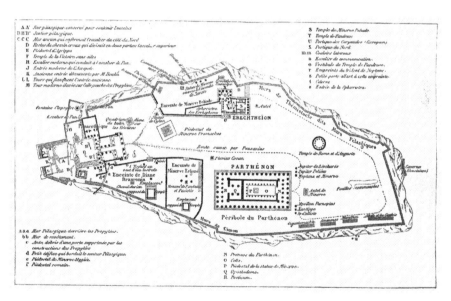

Old Map of Acropolis

There used to be a large fortress in Acropolis. But, today, all that's left are stone walls. But, you could still see the ruins of three grand structures – the Propylaea, the Erechtheion, and the great Parthenon.

The Propylaea is the grand entrance of the Acropolis. It was built to protect the ancient city from its enemies. It used to have five gates and it's supported by large Greek columns.

There's something about the Propylaea that's captivating. It makes you feel like you're entering a mystical world of beautiful Greek women, brave soldiers, and folklores.

The Erechtheion is an old temple located north of Acropolis. It's built for both Poseidon and Athena. This is one of the most elegant temples you'll ever see. It has a classic Ionic architecture. The columns are slender, and the carvings are intricate. This temple is still a beautiful and fascinating, so could just imagine how glorious it looked like during the ancient times.

Erechtheion

This temple has a room that houses the sacred olive wood statue of Athena. According to the myth, this statue was dropped from heaven. The most beautiful part of this building is the Porch of the Caryatids which features six statues of beautiful maidens functioning as columns. This is a proof of the ancient Greeks' creativity.

The most important temple on the Acropolis is the Parthenon. This striking temple was built in honor of the Goddess Athena – the patron of Athens. Parthenon literally means "an unmarried woman's apartment". It was believed that the goddess of strategy was a virgin.

This temple is made of marble. It has sophisticated architecture that's ahead of its time. It was completed in 432 BCE. The Parthenon has a classic Doric architecture (with a few Ionic elements). This means that the columns are thick and huge. This building is so stunning that it became the design inspiration for temples in Italy. It is also the design inspiration for many buildings in Washington, D.C., including the Jefferson Memorial, the National Gallery of Art, and the US Supreme Court.

The Temple of Olympian Zeus

Zeus was the supreme ruler of the sacred Mount Olympus. He was also known as the all-powerful god of war. He had two brothers – Poseidon (the god of the sea), and Hades (the god of the underworld). He was one of the greatest figures in Greek mythology, so it's no surprise that a number of temples were built in his honor.

The Temple of Olympian Zeus is about half a kilometer away from the Acropolis. It was built in 6th century BC, but it was completed in the

2nd century AD during the reign of the great Roman Emperor Hadrian.

The temple has gigantic Corinthian marble columns that will take your breath away. It's open for visitors from 8 am to 3 pm and the admission fee costs 6 euros. You can reach this temple via train (Akropolis, line 2).

The Ancient Agora of Athens

At the foot of the Acropolis, you'll find the Agora. This used to be the shopping mall of the ancient Athens.

Athenians regularly gathered here for three thousand years. It was the hub of ancient entrepreneurs and capitalists. It was the center of the city's economy. It was the foundation of Western economics, mathematics, and logic.

What's left of the Ancient Agora was turned into a museum. This museum showcases the sculptures and the artifacts found in the ancient marketplace. It is located at the restored Stoa of Attalos, the place where Socrates preaches about the virtue of temperance. It is also a place where Plato used to hang out. The Ancient Agora of Athens gives you a unique experience – it allows you to stand in the same ground where the greatest philosophers once stood.

Agora

This amazing marketplace used to be the center of Athenian politics, commerce, justice, and culture.

Aside from the museum, there are a lot of things that you can see in Ancient Agora, including:

- The Tower of the Winds – This marble clock tower was a horologion – a tool that ancient Greeks used to tell time. This tower was built by a Macedonian astronomer named Andronicus of Cyrrhus. This tower has interesting carvings and it has a number of features, including a wind vane, a water clock, and a sundials.

- The East Propylon – This is the eastern entrance of the Ancient Agora. It was built in 19 BC. Today, all that's left is a bunch of columns.

- Fethiye Mosque – This Ottoman mosque is a beautiful place of worship found at the northern part of the Ancient Agora. It's just a few steps from the Tower of the Winds. This Byzantine church was built in the 17th century and it has a stunning Ottoman architecture.

Syntagma Square

The Syntagma Square is open to the public. It is located at PI. Sintagmatos, Athens. It was named after the first Greek constitution. It has a grand fountain and it's surrounded by five-star hotels and shops. It's also the home of the stunning Parliament House.

The Parliament Building was built in 1836 and it was completed in 1842. It used to be the Royal Palace of King Otto. This building has a neoclassical architecture and it is probably one of the most beautiful buildings you'll ever see in your lifetime. There's something about this building that's intimidating and, at the same time, captivating. It symbolizes power and the great wealth Greece used to have.

Syntagma Square

You could also find a lot of stores in Syntagma Square including H &M and Nike, so it's a great place to shop.

Syntagma Square

The Panathenaic Stadium and the Olympic Stadium

Panathenaic Stadium

It's no secret that the Olympic Games started as a religious activity held in Olympia to honor the Greek god Zeus. This tradition started in 776 BC. This sporting competition was held every four years for almost 12 centuries.

The Panathenaic Stadium is a multi-purpose stadium located at Leof. Vasileos Konstantinou. It is a cultural monument and for many years, this stadium hosted track events involving nude male athletes.

The Panathenaic Stadium opened in 556 BC. It is also called Kallimarmaro, which means "made of marble". It was the site of the first ever Olympic Games in 1896.

This stadium is an architectural masterpiece. It is a testament of the excellent Greek craftsmanship.

Panathenaic Stadium

If you're more into modern sports arena, head to the Olympic Stadium. This magnificent stadium was built in 1980 and it was opened in 1982.

But, it was renovated in 2002 for the 2004 Olympic Games. It was no doubt one of the grandest Olympic Games in the history. The stadium has a football field and 9-lane race tracks. It has two electronic scoreboards. It is definitely one of the most beautiful stadiums in Europe.

The Olympic Stadium is also the site of many European and Greek sports competitions. Madonna held her concert at this huge Olympic Stadium in 2008.

6

Things That You Can Do Only in Athens

Most European cities look the same – they're filled with spectacular churches and magical palaces. But, Athens is different. You won't see fairytale like castles and elaborate fountains. You won't see the grand buildings that you're most likely to find in Krakow, Copenhagen, Serbia, and Paris. You won't see the medieval castles you can find in Wales, Bavaria, Prague, England, Dublin, and Edinburgh. But, there are also a few of awesome things that you can only do in Athens. Below is a list of the unique things that you can only do in Athens.

Explore the Vibrant Ancient Village of Plaka

Plaka is one of the most beautiful places you'll ever see. It is nestled in the northern and eastern slopes of the Acropolis It's quaint and colorful. It's definitely one of the most photogenic communities in the world. Every corner is picture perfect. This community is not open to cars, so you have to walk or bike around this neighborhood.

Plaka

Plaka is filled with vividly colored buildings and whimsical restaurants. The streets are lined with bright and vivid bougainvilleas. It's like you are transported to a different time or world. Plaka exudes nothing but good vibes! It is colorful and vivid. There's something about this neighborhood that's captivating – it can be the gleaming houses, the magnificent balconies decorated with flowers, or the quirky souvenir shops. But, whatever it is, there's something about Plaka that's truly magical.

This enchanting neighborhood is located on the slopes of a rocky mountain. This means that you have to climb stairs to explore the neighborhood. These stairs are lined with beautiful houses and cafes.

Plaka

Aside from the beautiful Cycladic houses, there are a lot of other things that you can see around this stunning neighborhood, such as:

1.Canellopoulos Museum

This museum showcases the vast art collection of the wealthy Canel-lopoulos Museum. It contains more than six thousand artifacts from prehistoric Greek civilization. It's also the home of a few modern artifacts. It's located at 12 Theorias Street, Plaka.

2.Anafiotika

This is a small neighborhood that's right under the Acropolis. This old town has breathtaking views. The houses in this neighborhood have a classic Cycladic architecture. This means that the houses have strong white walls and bright blue windows and doors. This neighborhood makes you feel like you're in a magical Greek island like Santorini or in Crete.

Anafiotika

3.Frissiras Museum

This museum is located on Kidathinaion Street. It has a fascinating neoclassical architecture that's easy on the eyes. It also houses over three thousand sculptures, drawings, and paintings.

Shop in an Ancient Flea Market Called Monastiraki

Monastiraki is one of the top shopping spots in Athens. It is a square that's has flea market stores, bargain shops, an Ottoman mosque, and an old Greek Church.

Monastiraki is a paradise for budget shoppers and treasure hunters. You can find beautiful and unique items at this flea market. You could find old books, sun glasses, furniture, second-hand clothes, fruits, accessories, figurines, jackets, furs, and even Greek flags.

This area is not only great for shopping, it's also good for sightseeing.

There are a number of historical sites in the area, including:

1.Hadrian's Library – Roman Emperor Hadrian had this built. The library was the home of rolls of papyrus. It used to have a reading room. But, today, it's just a bunch of walls and columns.

2.Church of Pantassa – This cathedral used to be attached to a monastery and it's facing the Monastiraki Station.

3.Tzistarakis Mosque – This beautiful mosque was built in 1759. It has a classic Ottoman architecture filled with arches and domes. It used to be a worship house, a storehouse, and a prison. But, it's now used as a museum showcasing the Greek Folk Art.

Tzistarakis Mosque

Meditate in the Athens National Garden

The Athens National Garden is located at Amalias 1, Athens. It's just a few steps away from the Syntagma Square. This garden is a lot simpler than other European gardens. It's peaceful and quiet – perfect for meditation. It has more than seven thousand trees and more than four thousand bushes. It's a paradise for nature lovers and botanists. This garden is the home of unique plants including the Canary Island date palms and the Chinese "trees of heaven".

This garden has six lakes with swans and ducks. If you're tired of walking around the busy city all day, this garden is your perfect escape.

Climb the Lycabettus Hill

The Lycabettus Hill (or Mount Lycabettus) is one of the popular tourist spots in Athens. It is the home of the Lykovatias Forest. It's 277 meters above the ground, making it one of the highest spots in the city. According to a legend, the goddess Athena carried the rock from Pentelis to the Acropolis. But, before she reached the ancient mountain, she heard that two of her servants opened the basket containing an infant named Erichthonius (which would later become a king). Athena was so mad that she dropped the rock. The rock later became the Lycabettus Hill.

This limestone rock has a theatre and a restaurant. It also has an amphitheater which was the venue of the concerts of well-known international artists like Vanessa Mae, the Pet Shop Boys, James Brown, Bjork, and Tracy Chapman.

This stunning hill is also the home of the Church of St. George. This church has a pure white exterior, but it has a colorful interior. The ceiling is decorated with beautiful paintings and an elegant chandelier. It's something that you should take time to see.

But, what makes the hill special is not the church or the theatre – it's the breathtaking panoramic view of the Acropolis and the entire city.

You can get to this hill by driving a car, there's a parking space next to the theatre. You can also climb up the hill on foot or if you're not into hiking, you can take the cable car.

Cruise Around the Islands of Poros, Hydra, and Aegina from Athens

One of the great things about Athens is that it's just a few hours away from beautiful Greek Islands. It's no secret that Greece is the home of some of the most fabulous beaches in the world. If you're a certified beach lover, you should take a day trip to the Saronic Islands - Aegina, Hydra, and Poros.

Hydra

Hydra is just two hours away from Athens via the Port of Piraues. This small Saronic Island is dazzling and ravishing. All you could see is yellow, green, and blue. It has picturesque villages and relaxing beaches. It's one of the popular day trips from Athens.

It was once the home of the notorious Saronic pirates. One of the special things about this island is that cars are generally not allowed, so you have to explore it by foot.

Spetses is one of the breathtaking Saronic Islands. It is approximately an hour and forty-five minutes from Athens. It's known for its rock buildings, green mountains, and captivating blue waters.

Aegina is three hours from Athens and it has stunning views that will definitely take your breath away. It's also the home of the stunning Temple of Aphaea.

Aegina

You can visit one of these islands if you decide to do the daytrip on your own. But, a lot of travel agencies offer day cruises to these three islands from Athens. So, to make the best out of your trip, it's good to take a day cruise to these three islands. You could find a lot of day cruise boats at the Port of Piraues, but it's still best to book ahead online or by phone.

Statue of Apollo

7

Top 5 Affordable Hotels in Hotels

Athens is a popular tourist spot, so it's filled with grand and luxurious hotels. Most of these hotels have rooftop pools overlooking the Acropolis. These hotels have extravagant spas, gyms, restaurants, and bars. The rooms are so grandiose that they make you feel like a royalty. But, these hotels can cost an arm and a leg.

Fortunately, Athens is also filled with homey, amazing, and affordable hotels. Below is the list of the best budget friendly hotels in the "city of the violent crown".

The Stanley

The Stanley Athens has a captivating modern exterior. Rooms are complete with modern amenities. The rooms have a good view of the Acropolis. This hotel also has a few function rooms that are perfect for conferences, seminars, parties, and weddings.

This four-star hotel is situated in a busy and touristy area. It's just a few steps away from the Metaxourgeio Metro Station. It's located at Odysseos 1 – Karaiskaki Sq, Athens. And the best thing about this hotel is that it's affordable. You could stay in this luxurious hotel for only $69 a night.

Phone: +30 21 1990 0900

Hermes Hotel

Hermes Hotel is located at the heart of the busy Plaka neighborhood. It is located at Apollonos 19, just a few steps from the Acropolis. This modern three-star hotel is classy, comfortable, and easy on the eyes. It has a roof garden, a cozy lounge, and stunning restaurant that serves continental dishes. The hotel offers free Wi-Fi. It also has a bar and a playroom. They offer a breakfast buffet, too.

The rooms are cozy, warm, and comfortable and they all have immaculate marble bathrooms. This hotel has excellent service and affordable prices. Rooms cost at least $83 a night. This hotel is perfect for those who want to spend a lot of time in Plaka.

Phone: +30 21 0322 2706

Polis Grand Hotel

Polis Grand Hotel has a modern and hip exterior. The rooms are so cozy that they almost make you feel like you're at home. Its balcony restaurant overlooks the Acropolis and gives you a good panoramic view of this stunning city. It's perfect for romantic dates. It serves buffet breakfast.

This four-star hotel is located at 19 Patision and 10 Veranzerou St., Athens. It's affordable, too. Hotel rooms cost at least $84.70.

Phone: +30 21 0524 3156

Socrates

The Socrates Hotel is located at Neofytou Metaxa 27 – 29, Athens. This three-star hotel has an easy access to the tourist neighborhood of Plaka. It's a few minutes from the Parthenon and the Acropolis. It's also a short walk away from the Omonoia Square and Monastiraki traditional market.

This quaint hotel has interesting walls that's look good on your Instagram feed. It also has a great bar and a "24/7" room service. It's affordable, too. You can book a twin or double room for as low as $40.60.

Phone: +30 21 0884 2211

Attalos Hotel

Attalos Hotel has an eclectic façade and a simple exterior. It is just one hundred meter from the Monastiraki Train Station. It has comfortable and elegant rooms. It has a breakfast buffet area and a rooftop bar where you could witness the glory of the Acropolis. It is just a five-minute walk to Ermou, the busiest shopping street in Athens.

Attalos Hotel is located at 29 Athinas Street, Athens. It's a touristy neighborhood lined with stores and quaint shops. This three-star hotel is just amazing and it's affordable, too. You can book a room for as low as $57.

To get the best rates, you should book ahead. It's also wise to visit Athens during off-peak season (autumn or early spring).

Phone: +30 21 0321 2801

8

The Greek Gastronomical Experience: The Top Five Restaurants in Athens

There's something about Greek food that keeps you begging for more. Greek dishes are delicious and healthy. It's filled with seafoods, fishes, and vegetables. You could try various dishes like Amygdalota,

Baklava, Bougatsa, Courgette Balls, Galaktoboureko, and of course, the famous Greek Salad.

Athens has a string of fabulous restaurants that cater to every taste and budget. Below is the list of the top 5 restaurants that you should visit while in Greece.

Funky Gourmet

This restaurant has two Michelin stars. It is recognized as one of the best restaurants in the world. It is a hip, modern restaurant located in Paramithias, Gazi. This place is perfect for those who like Mediterranean food. The Funky Gourmet serves creative and out of this world dishes such as a fish fillet dipped in white chocolate and exotic lobster. The restaurant opened in 2007 and it has been on fire since. Meals usually cost $150, a bit pricey. But, it's all worth it.

The Funky Gourmet exudes elegance and opulence. It's innovative and it has a glass ceiling that gives you a good view of the sky. The food presentation is just amazing, and the desserts are too pretty to eat. Don't forget to make a reservation before heading to Athens.

Address: 13 Paramithias str
  Phone: +30 21 0524 2727

Strofi

The best thing about Strofi is that it gives you a good view of the Acropolis. It's located in Rovertou Galli. This restaurant serves authentic Greek and Mediterranean cuisine. It has an impressive wine list, too. It was established in 1975 and it has been one of the most popular restaurants in Athens since then.

Strofi serves delicious food at an affordable price. Don't forget to try the fried feta cheese, steak in oregano sauce, and cheese baked eggplant.

Address:Rovertou Galli 25
   Phone:+30 21 0921 4130

The Old Tavern of Psarras

The Old Tavern of Psarras is one of the few touristy restaurants where Greeks dine. So, if you want to eat like a local, head to this place. This romantic restaurant has an outdoor area that leads to the Acropolis.

Psarras serve authentic Greek traditional cuisine. Don't miss the chance to try the classic Greek salad and stuffed vine.

Address: Erechtheos 16
   Phone:+30 210 3218734

Varoulko

This seaside restaurant has everything you could ever ask for – good food and breathtaking views. This restaurant is located in Akti Koumoundourou, Mikrolimano. It serves delicious seafood soups, garlic shrimps, and eggplant salad. Varoulko has that breezy Greek ambiance that exudes nothing but good vibes.

Address: Akti Koumoundourou 52
   Phone:+30 21 0522 8400

Spondi

Spondi is a luxury two Michelin star restaurant located in Pyrronos 5, Pagkrati. It has a classic Mediterranean interior with whitewashed rock walls and interesting chandeliers. It's great for dates and anniversaries. The restaurant also has an outdoor dining area where guests can enjoy good food and the cold breeze of Athenian wind.

Spondi opened in 1996 and founded by well-known Greek chef Apostolos Trastelis. It's a bit pricey (a full meal would cost about $100), but it's worth every cent. This restaurant serves interesting dishes, such as Wild Mushroom Foie Grass, Chocolate Coeur de Guanaja, and Lobster served with peaches, potatoes, and tarragon. They also have top notch customer service.

Address: Pirronos 5
   Phone:+30 21 0756 4021

9

The Best Athenian Museums

The Acropolis and the historic center of Athens look like open-air museums. They are relics of the past. But, if you want to know more about the ancient Greek civilization, you should visit a few of the city's many museums. Here are the best 5:

Acropolis Museum

The Acropolis is, no doubt, the eternal symbol of Athens. It is an ancient city that sits on top of a rocky mountain. It is one of the most historical, glorious, and magnificent landmarks in the world. It is 150 meters above the ground, so you can see this glorious ancient metropolis from almost anywhere in Athens.

Acropolis Museum

If you want to know more about this ancient city, head to the New Acropolis Museum. This modern building looks nothing like the museums in Rome, Berlin, Paris, or Prague. It has a modern architecture that showcases the mathematical precision of ancient Greece. But, it houses the most magnificent and historical artworks made in the ancient city of Acropolis.

The museum was opened in 2009. It was designed by a well-known Swiss architect named Bernard Tschumi. There's something mysterious and captivating about this amazing museum. It has glass walls, so you could enjoy the view of the Acropolis while you're in the museum.

This modern museum is built on the site of an ancient archaeological city called Makrygianni neighborhood. You could still see the remains of this marvelous ancient neighborhood from the huge opening on the museum's entrance hall. You can also see this fascinating archaeological site through the glass floors of the museum interior. The Makrygianni neighborhood is a testament of how beautiful ancient Athens was. This relic captures about three thousand years of Athenian life.

The museum has permanent exhibitions, namely:

- **The Gallery of the Slopes of the Acropolis.**This is gallery is the first art exhibition you'll find in the museum. It showcases sculptures, artifacts, bath vases, decorative motifs, figurines, and perfume bottles from two sanctuaries located on the slopes of the sacred mountain – the ancient temple of Dionysos Eleuthereus and the Sanctuary of the Asclepios, a temple dedicated to Nymphe.

- **The Archaic Acropolis Gallery** .This is a three-dimensional exhibit. This means that you can see the artworks from all sides. The Archaic Acropolis Gallery showcases the ancient Athenian artworks from the Archaic period (7 BC to 480 BC).The artworks in this gallery are just exquisite and hauntingly beautiful. It's like you're transported to a different time and place. These artworks are proof that even in 7th BC, Athens has already a thriving economy and a rich intellectual and creative life. This wonderful city is definitely ahead of its time.

- **The Parthenon Gallery** .During its peak, Parthenon was popular as one of the most beautiful and powerful temples in the world.The Parthenon Gallery showcases the ancient artworks and scriptural decorations of this popular landmark.

- **The Artifacts of Propylaia, Athena Nike, and Erechtheion.** This gallery showcases the artworks of the main entrance of the Parthenon called Propylaia. This grand entrance housed magnificent sculptures by well-known artists such as Alkamekes. This gallery also houses the statues from other famous temples, such as the Erechtheion and Athena Nike.

- **From 5th CB to 5th AD** .There's something about this gallery that's haunting and captivating. You could walk amidst the ancient sculptures placed on marble pedestals. This gallery showcases the artworks from the Sanctuary of Artemis Brauronia. This part of the museum also houses popular artworks such as the portrait of Alexander the Great by Leochares. You could also find the statue of Prokne, the daughter of King Pandion of Attica and the statues of countless emperors, generals, orators, priests, and philosophers.

The Acropolis Museum is located at Dionysiou Areopagitou 15. It is open from 8 am to 8 pm during summer season (except on Mondays – the museum closes at 4 pm). During winter season, the museum is open from 9 am to 5 pm on most days. The entrance fee costs 5 euros.

Address:Dionysiou Areopagitou 15
   Phone: +30 21 0900 0900

Benaki Museum

This museum was established in 1930 and it's housed inside the beautiful Benaki Museum located at Koumpari I, Athens. It's right across the National Garden. It was established in 1930 by famous Greek art collector Antonis Benakis in honor of his entrepreneur and politician father Emmanouil Benakis.

This museum has a classic architecture. But, when you go inside, you feel like you're transported to a time of extravagant dresses and lavish furniture.

Benakis Museum

The Benaki Museum has a wide collection of elaborate costumes. It also showcases the paintings of famous artists, such as Theodoros, Ioannis Permeniatis, El Greco, Michael Damaskenos, Emmanuel Tzanes, Nikolaos Kantounis, and Dionysios Solomos. It also features artworks and artifacts from Anatolia, Egypt, Arabian Peninsula, the Middle East, Persia, Mesopotamia, India, Sicily, Spain, and North Africa.

This museum has pure white walls and a number of amazing chandeliers. It houses more than 40,000 artworks and artifacts. It also has a museum souvenir shop and a snack bar that gives you a good view of the Parthenon.

The Benaki Museum is open from 10 am to 6 pm every Wednesdays and Fridays from 10 am to midnight every Thursdays and Saturdays. It is open from 10 am to 4 pm on Sundays and closed every Monday and Tuesday. The entrance fee costs 9 euros.

Address:Koumpari 1
   Phone:+30 21 0367 1000

National Archaeological Museum

National Archaeological Museum

The National Archaeological Museum is the home of the most important archaeological artifacts in Greece from the prehistoric period to until the late antiquity (8 A.D.). It was established by Greek governor Ioannis Kaposdistrias.

This museum has a neoclassical Greek architecture. The building's façade is filled with intimidating columns. It has an impressive collection of gold artifacts, including the Mask of Agamemnon, Mycenean gold cups, and elliptical funeral head dresses. This museum is like a large treasure chest.

The National Archaeological is a paradise for Greek mythology fans. You could find stunning and ethereal statues of Greek gods and goddesses Zeus, Athena, Themis, Aphrodite, Asklepius, Dionysos, Pan, Eros, and Satyr. These statues are so beautiful that they look like they're floating on the exquisite marble floor.

You could also find a number of painted jars that depicted ancient war scenes and a huge bronze statue of a jockey riding a horse. Everything in this museum is absolutely magnificent and captivating.

This museum is located at 28is Oktovriou 44. It is open from 12 noon to 8 pm on Sundays and Mondays. It is open from Tuesday to Saturday from 8 am to 8 pm. The entrance fee costs 10 euros.

Address:28is Oktovriou 44
  Phone:+30 21 3214 4800

Goulandris Museum of Cycladic Art

This museum has a mansion-like interior. It's housed in the Stathatos Mansion - one of Athens architectural gems. Its exterior exudes elegance and opulence. This museum is a great place to discover the spellbinding Greek history. We all know the Cycladic architecture – it's used all over Santorini. But, if you want to know more about Cycladic art, head to the Goulandris Museum.

The Goulandris Museum is known for its vast collect of Cycladic art – figurines that were created in the Aegan Islands during 3000 BC or the early "bronze age", the height of the Cyclandic culture.

You could find a lot of interesting minimalistic Cycladic marble sculptures produced during the Neolithic Period. Some of these sculptures look like violins, but in fact they are symbols of naked squatting women. These artworks symbolize the Ancient Greek's talent, culture, and creativity. These pieces of arts are carefully arranged in glass-protected installations. This museum magically fuses the old with the new.

This museum has different sections, namely:

1.Cycladic Art Collection

This section houses the most important Cycladic art collection in the world. It showcases nude marble statues that inspired artists like Henry Moore, Barbara Hepworth, Giacometti, Modigliani, and Brancusi.

2.Ancient Greek Art: History in Images

This section showcases the history of the Aegean societies. It features artworks and artifacts that symbolize the political, cultural, techno-logical, and social development of Greek civilization. You would see jars, busts, warrior helmets, and other interesting artifacts.

3.Cyprus: Aspects of Ancient Art and Culture

This section showcases the ancient artifacts and sculptures from Cyprus. The artworks are rather interesting and thought provoking. This part of the museum also contains unique and intriguing treasures and jars from Cyprus – the island of Aphrodite. These artifacts are usually made of glass, gold, clay, silver, and bronze. Most of these artworks are part of the art collection of a wealthy Cyprian named Thanos Zintilis.

4.Scenes From The Daily Life in Antiquity

This is probably the most beautiful and interesting part of the Goulandris Museum. It showcases over 150 artifacts from Ancient Greece, including weapons, vases, and figurines. These artworks are divided into three five parts or themes – the Underworld, the World of Men, Eros, Gods, and Heroes.

The Goulandris Museum also has a temporary exhibition area where known artists like Sarah Lucas, Thomas Struth, Louise Bourgeois, Ai Weiwei, and Martin Kippenberger display their works.

This dazzling museum is located in Neofitou Douka 4, Athens. The entrance fee costs 7 euros (as of writing). It's open from 11 am to 9 pm on Sunday. It is also open from 10 am to 5 pm every Monday, Wednesday, and Saturday. It's open from 11 am to 8 pm on Thursdays and it is closed every Tuesday.

Address: Neofitou Douka 4
   Phone:+30 21 0722 8321

Numismatic Museum of Athens

The Numismatic Museum is not as popular as the other museums in this list. But, it's a place you should not miss if you're in Athens. This museum has a fascinating Beaux-Arts architecture. It almost looks like a modern palace.

The museum interior has interesting designs and colors. The Byzantine and Christian paintings on the building's museum are captivating. This museum has one of the biggest collections of ancient coins. You could find rare and valuable coins and gems, including the gold coins of Epidaurus, Ancient Corinth, Sicily, and Byzantine Empire. These coins bear the image of kings, rulers, gods, and goddesses.

The exhibition rooms are exquisite and fascinating. These rooms look like they're part of a lavish European palace. This museum is a haven for coin collectors. But, it's also a paradise for book lovers. The museum has over twelve thousand books about archaeology, numismatics, and history.

The museum area also has a stunning garden with fascinating statues. It's a good place to just walk around and think about the good things in life.

The Numismatic Museum was founded in 1838, making it one of the oldest museums in Greece. It is located at Ilou Melatron, Eleftheriou Venizelou 12, Athens. It's open from 9 am to 4 am from Tuesday to Sunday. It's open from 1 pm to 8 pm every Monday. The entrance fee costs 6 euros.

Address:Eleftheriou Venizelou 12
  Phone:+30 21 0363 2057

10

Exploring the Greek Art Scene: The Best Art Galleries

The contemporary Greek art is rather captivating and mind-puzzling. If you're into eclectic (and classic) art, you should check out the art galleries around Athens.

Ileana Tounta Contemporary Art Centre

This art gallery was founded in 1988 and it's the home of various contemporary artworks in Athens. This gallery has a simple industrial space that's decorated with interesting and thought provoking art.

The Ilean Tounta Contemporary Art Centre sometimes features the work of eclectic artists like Dimitrios Antonitsis, Eva Mitala, Katerina Kotsala, Frini Mouzakitou, and Ionna Pantazopoulou.

Address: Klefton 48

Deste Foundation for Contemporary Art

Deste Foundation is a gallery established by Dakis Joannou. This art gallery has an interesting exterior. This art gallery showcases odd and sometimes, mind-boggling art installations. You could also find a few paintings and photographs. This gallery is for those looking unique and eclectic art.

Address: Filellinon 11, Nea Ionia

Rebecca Camhi Gallery

This beautiful gallery is definitely one of the most beautiful and popular galleries in Athens. It was established in 1995 and it's housed in a stunning neoclassical building located in Leonidou 9. This gallery showcases the works of international artists like Nobuyoshi Araki, Rita Akermann, and Nan Goldin. It also showcases the work of famous Greek artists.

Address: Leonidou 9

CAN - Christina Androulidaki Gallery

This classy art space is located at Panagiotuo Anagnostopoulou 42, Athen. CAN was founded by Christina Androulidaki who has art and history degrees from the University of Edinburgh and the Courtauld Institute in London. This gallery is filled with white spaces that showcase the work of Maria Kriara, Lefteris Tapas, Alexis Vasilikos, Dimitris Condos, and Marianna Ignataki.

Address: Panagiotou Anagnostopoulou 42

Radio Athenes

This amazing museum was founded in 2014 by Andreas Melas and Helena Papadopoulos. It's a non-profit contemporary art gallery. It's located at the heart of the city, at 15 Petraki, Athens. It is also a bookstore and an event hall. The installations can be viewed from the outside with its clear glass wall. A lot of artists hang out here to find inspiration for painting and writing.

Address:Street, Petraki 15

11

Experience the Greek Coffee Culture: Best Coffee Shops in Athens

The Greek coffee (locally known as ellinikos kafes) is a powdered ground coffee served in half cups. It's a lot stronger than the regular coffee and it's brewed in a pot called briki. The baristas usually use a utensil called kaimaki to create foam. Coffee is a vital part of the Greek culture. It was used to predict the weather during the ancient times. Greeks believe that if the bubbles are clustered in the middle of the cup, it's going to be a sunny day. If the bubbles form around the mouth of the cup, it's going to rain. Also, frappe was invented in Greece during the 60s.

Today, the Athens is filled with fascinating and modern coffee shops. Some of these cafes even have world class bartenders. Below is a list of the best coffee shops in the city.

Tailor Made

Tailor Made is one of the first specialty coffee shops in Athens. It's located in Plateia Agias Eirinis that serves fresh roasted coffee from different parts of the world, including Ethiopia, Kenya, Brazil, Panama, Honduras, and Costa Rica. It also serves delicious home-made desserts, infusions, snacks, and teas. It's a good place to hang out. This café has an in-house DJ, too.

Tailor Made has a funky and electrifying urban interior that's cool and relaxing. The ambience is superb and the coffee is even more amazing.

Address: Agias Irinis 2
  Phone: +30 21 3004 9645

Chaplin

Chaplin is one of those side street coffee shops around Athens.

Chaplin is one of the city's highest rated coffee shops and for a good reason. It has an interesting interior that's usually filled with Earth colors. It also has a photogenic giant chandelier that's perfect for your Instagram feed. It also has an outdoor seating area perfect for people watching. This shop serves great coffee and superfood cocktails.

Address: Kalamiotou 16
   Phone:+30 698 745 4777

The Underdog

The Underdog is located at Iraklidon 8. The coffee so good and it is the workplace award-winning barista named Michalis Dimitrakopoulus. This café has an interesting interior, a clean coffee bar, and delightful wooden stools. They serve cold beers, too. It's a perfect place to hang out.

Address: Iraklidon 8
   Phone:+30 21 3036 5393

Taf Coffee

If you love coffee art, head to Taf Coffee located at Emmanouil Mpenaki 7. It was founded by Yiannis Taloumis in the 90s. This shop serves an award-winning espresso blend called Rosebud. Like the Underdog, Tag Coffee has an award-winning team, too. Their iced brew coffee is to die for. This coffee shop has become so successful that it has opened branches in Milan, London, and Singapore.

Address: Emmanouil Benaki 7
   Phone:+30 21 0380 0014

Mind The Cup

Mind The Cup is a quaint little café located in Peristeri. If you want some quiet time, head to this place. It's pleasantly located away from the busy touristy streets. It has a funky street interior that will surely captivate your interest.

Mind The Cup is one of the best places to relax and just hang out. It has a great interior and it offers outdoor seating, too. The baristas are super friendly and then sometimes have a DJ, too.

Address:Emiliou Veaki 29
  Phone:+30 21 0577 6010

12

The Best Bars in the City

Greeks have a sophisticated taste. So, it's not surprising that the city is filled with classy, elegant, and interesting bars.

The night life in Athens is just as fascinating as its temples and historic sites. Below is a list of the best bars in the city.

Brettos

Established in 1909, Brettos is the oldest surviving bar in Athens and definitely one of the most beautiful bars you'll ever visit in your lifetime. Its walls are decorated with colorful bottles of wine and beer. The bar also features barrels of perfectly age wine.

The place serves two hundred fifty different cocktails and a hundred seventy Greek wines. It's definitely a paradise for picky beer drinkers and wine connoisseurs. This bar is located in Kidathineon 41, Athens. It's in the quaint and colorful Plaka neighborhood.

Phone:+30 21 0323 2110

Galaxy Bar

If you like good wine and you have a lot of money to burn, head to the Galaxy Bar. This bar is nestled on the top floor of Hilton Hotel in Athens. It allows you to drink a kick-ass cocktail while staring at the grandeur of the Acropolis.

The Galaxy Bar has an impressive wine list and stunning views. It's a great place to socialize or just enjoy a glass of exquisite wine.

This elegant bar is located at 46 Vassilissis Sofias Avenue, Athens. It is open from 7:30 pm until early morning.

Phone:+30 21 0728 1402

Seven Jokers

This elegant bar is a favorite after-work hangout area of many local young professionals. It's a place where hard-working millennials drink cold beer and eat finger foods after a long day at work. This bar is so beautiful that it feels like you're transported to the 1920s. Its walls are decorated with expensive wines. You could see elegant and colorful lamps hanging from the ceiling. This bar also has friendly and energetic bartenders and an impressive wine list.

You should visit this Instagram-worthy bar while in Athens. It's located at Voulis 7 and it's open from 6 pm until early in the morning.

Phone:+30 21 0321 9225

A For Athens Bar

A For Athens is a hip urban hotel next to the Monastriki train station. Its bar is becoming one of the best and most popular night hangouts in the city. This rooftop bar has the best view of the Acropolis.

The A for Athens Bar has friendly bartenders who serve fascinating cocktails with interesting names. Its head bartender, Theodore Pyrillos, was hailed the champion of the European Cocktail Competition.

This bar has a vibrant and vivid atmosphere that draws a long queue of guests each night. So, it's best to make a reservation.

Phone:+30 21 0324 4244
  Address:Miaouli 2

The Clumsies

The Clumsies is known as one of the best bars in the world. It is housed inside a beautiful neoclassical building. It has an elegant interior and a team of world class bartenders. This bar serves "out of this world" cocktails that will give you a unique experience. These cocktails are not only delicious, they're also innovative and picture perfect.

This bar is open as early as 10 am and closes at 2 am. It is located in Praxitelous, Athens.

Phone:+30 21 0323 2682
   Address:Praxitelous 30

13

Party Like A Greek: The Best Night Clubs in Athens

Greeks are nice, polite, and friendly people. They are energetic, and they love to have a good time. So, it's no surprise that Athens has an electrifying energetic nightlife. Below is the list of the night clubs that you should not miss in Athens.

Island

Island is one the most popular night clubs in Athens. It is the hub of jet-setting celebrities, socialites, and stylish locals. This club has a restaurant that serves the best international cuisines and inventive cocktails. It's definitely a place where you could dance and relax. It's a good place to meet new people, too.

This is located on Sounio Avenue, Variza, Athens Riviera, about 27 kilometers from downtown Athens.

Lohan Nightclub

Lohan Nightclub is one of the hottest nightclubs in Athens and yes, it's owned by Lindsay Lohan. It is located at 30, Iera Odos 32 and it's definitely one of the wildest clubs in the city. This club is a hedonist's paradise, a feast for the senses. You could see "black light" dancers, sexy vixens, and attractive party animals everywhere. The club features famous Greek DJs, too. It's a good place to cut loose and have a good time.

Phone: +30 698 750 1825

Dybbuk

Dybbuk exudes nothing but good vibes. It has a great combination of hypnotizing music and spectacular lights. It has been the center of Athens nightlife since 2009. It's located at the posh Loulkiano Street. It is the home of famous DJs like Agent Greg. This club also hosts dance shows every now and then.

There's something about Dybbuk that's electrifying and captivating. It is a great place to meet new people, too.

Bolivar Beach Bar

Bolivar Beach Bar is located on Poseidonos Avenue, Alimos. It's just 30 minutes away from the tourism center of Athens. This bar combines the best things in life – the beach, good music, good food, sun, cold beer, and beautiful people. It's the ultimate party destinations for tourists and Greek millenials. This place has amazing tiki huts and mind-blowing cocktails.

Phone: +30 697 036 7684

Steam

Steam is vibrant, energetic, and vivacious, just like the Athenian nightlife. This club is the site of many events and parties. It has an impressive list of amazing DJs, including Amalia Kalameniou and the Cosmic Boys. This club plays hypnotic music that makes you forget all your worries for a few hours.

Steam is located at Evrimedontos 3, Gazi and just a few steps away from the Karameikos Train Station.

Phone: +30 21 0341 2120

14

The Ultimate 3 Day Athens Travel Itinerary

Athens is the center of the Ancient Greece. It is filled with remnants of its rich cultural past. The city is the home to picturesque neighborhoods, jaw-dropping views, fascinating old temples, and stunning mosques. There are a lot of sites to visit, so below is a three-day travel itinerary that you can use to plan your trip:

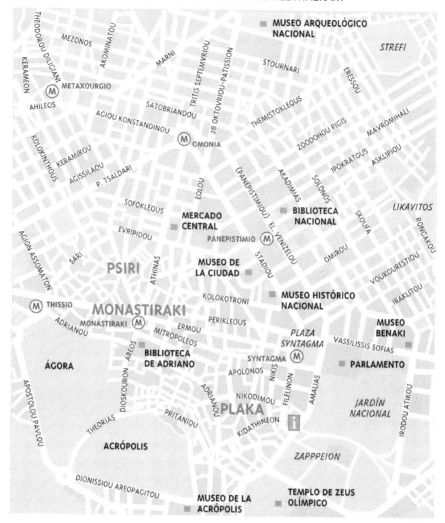

Day 1- The Acropolis, Plaka, and Nearby Tourist Sites

- 1.Visit the Acropolis and its temples – the Propylaia, the Parthenon, the Temple of Athena Nike, and the Erechtheion.
- 2.Explore the ancient neighborhood of Plaka.
- 3.See the Ancient Agora.

- 4.Visit the Syntagma Square.
- 5.Meditate at the National Garden.
- 6.Shop at the Monastiraki market.
- 7.See the Acropolis Museum

Day 2 – Museums and the Lycabettus Hill

- 1.Visit the National Archaelogical Museum.
- 2.See the Benaki Museum.
- 3.Explore the Goulandris Museum of Cycladic Art.
- 4.Climb the Lycabettus Hill.

Lycabettus Hill

Day 3 – Day Trip to the Saronic Island

Take a day trip to the Saronic Islands of Hydra, Aegina, and Poros, especially if you're not planning to visit another Greek city or Island (Santorini, Crete, etc). These islands are just as stunning as the more popular Greek islands.

Aegina

If you have more time, take day trips to Cape Sounion, Olympia, and Meteora so you could see more fascinating temples and other tourist spots. Join discounted group tours. If you're a foodie, you can also join the classic Athens food tour. And most of all, if you're already in Athens, why not extend your stay in Greece and visit the stunning Mykonos or Santorini?

Hydra

15

Conclusion

I hope that this book was able to help you plan a hassle-free and fun trip to Athens. Before traveling to Athens, here's a list of things that you should keep in mind:

- Before you travel, make sure that you have complete travel documents. Also, make sure that you have the contact number of your country's embassy in Greece.
- Book your hotel and ferry tickets ahead to get great deals.
- Use Booking.com to get great hotel discounts.
- Greece is a smoking country. So, you'll probably see people smoking anywhere.
- You can see stray animals anywhere. This can be a bit annoying for tourists.
- Don't forget to bring your camera – Athens is one of the most photogenic cities in the world.
- Invest in a good map. This will make your life easier.
- Take time to learn a few Greek phrases.
- Make sure that you have enough euros in your pocket. A lot of stores in Athens do not accept credit cards.
- Make sure that you are appropriately dressed before you enter a

church.

- Pack light if you are traveling to another Greek island through ferry. Use a backpack. It's easier to carry around.
- Be kind. Greeks are kind people, but only if you're nice to them, too.
- Don't hesitate to ask for help.
- Be wary of scams.
- Most ATMs in Greece have a daily withdrawal limit.
- Don't forget to try Gyros (Greek shawarma-like snack) and the Kalamari (fried octopus).
- The tap water in Athens is generally safe. But, if you go out of Athens, drink bottled water.
- Always wear your seatbelt when you're in the car. Greeks are crazy drivers.
- You will need to pay toll fees if you're visiting multiple towns.
- Pharmacies are closed during weekends. So, make sure you have all the medicine you'll need before the weekend.
- Drink a lot of water when you're in Athens, especially during summer time.
- A lot of Greek taverns do not have a closing time. They close when the last customer leaves!
- Check the inclusion of your hotel accommodation. A lot of hotels in Athens do not offer free breakfast.
- Greeks get annoyed when tourists publicly display their drunkenness, so it's important to drink moderately.
- Most road signs are written in Greek, so it's not advisable for tourists to rent a car and drive. Use public transportation instead.
- Take a day trip from Athens if you have more time.

16

SANTORINI INTRODUCTION

Santorini is a favorite destination – not just for people in Greece but also for people all over the world. Unfortunately, there are so many places and things to do in Santorini that even planning a vacation to the island can be a lot of work.

Where do you go first?

What food should you taste?

What should you do?

By the end of this book, you should have fairly good idea of what to do and the places to visit in Santorini for a truly satisfying vacation.

17

Brief History And Background

Santorini is rumored to be the location of the famous City of Atlantis – and it's not surprising why. The island is actually a remnant of a volcanic caldera – which makes it amazing in itself. A volcanic caldera is essentially a volcanic crater that was formed after an eruption, causing the mouth of the volcano to collapse.

Found in the Southern Portion of the Aegean Sea, Santorini forms part of the Cyclades group of islands. What's interesting here is that while the island is globally known as "Santorini", its official name is actually Thera or Thira – hence the Airport in the island is called the Thira International Airport.

The municipality of Santorini is comprised of 6 islands. There's Santorini and Therasia – both of which are inhabited. Three of the islands are uninhabited which include Nea Kameni, Palaia Kameni, Aspronisi, and Christiana. Within the inhabited islands, you can find several major settlements which include Fira, Oia, Emporio, Kamari, Perissa, Imerovigli, Pygros, and Therasia.

Volcanic Eruption

While there are definitely lots of interesting things relating to Santorini, the fact of its creation is perhaps the most important thing to consider. It was built overtime as a volcano is slowly and repeatedly constructed around the sides. When the caldera or the top portion eventually collapsed inwards, the remaining land formed what is now the famous Santorini.

You can probably picture a volcano and easily imagine the topmost portion being shaved off, representing the collapsed part of the mouth. However, you'd think that the main town of Santorini would be located on the bottom-flat surface, which isn't the case at all. The town is situated on the top portion – which is why you'll find that almost all hotels offer a bird's eye view of the Aegean Sea – that's perfectly natural considering the elevation of the town itself.

Now you'd probably want to ask – is there a chance of another volcanic eruption happening on Santorini? While the volcano in Santorini is dormant, it's not exactly inactive. Hence, there's still a chance of the volcano erupting at some point in time. The question is: when? There are a group of scientists today that are tasked with the constant monitoring of Santorini's volcano so that if it eventually happens, it would be easy to warn people about it.

Of course, that's not something you have to worry about during a vacation in the area.

SANTORINI - GREECE

Villages and Towns

There are actually lots of towns in Santorini, each one capable of offering you something unique. While you might not be able to visit all these villages, it helps to find out which ones offer you the activity you want.

- Fira – situated on the top of the cliff, Fira offers a spectacular sunset on a daily basis. It's the center of Santorini, especially during the tourist season when all the visitors flock to the village for some much-needed rest and relaxation. You'll find that most hotels are situated in Fira.

- Karterados – around 2 kilometers away from Fira, Karterados is most famous for its unique architecture. While Fira itself offers a series of stunning buildings, Karterados is the places you want to visit for Instagram-worthy pictures.

- Oia or Ia – a place you should definitely visit for its sunrise or sunset, Oia is perched on top of the caldera. Of course, you can watch the sunrise or sunset anywhere on the island, but Oia is definitely the best place to be in for those events.

- Kamari – best known for the black pebble beach, this particular village is situated on the lower portion of the island. The word "black pebble" is not just a fancy term – the sand is literally done in black pebbles resulting from the volcanic eruption.

- Imerovigli – just a few minutes away from Fira by bus, this small town is also known for its sunsets and sunrise. If you can't go to Oia, you'll have just as much fun in Imerovigli.

- Pyrgos – this is the highest point on the island, containing beautiful monasteries that looks good from any angle. Most people say that Pyrgos can compete with Oia when it comes to sunsets.

- Firostefani – a 10-minute walk away from Fira, you can easily visit the village and take advantage of its unique view of the volcano.

- Perissa – most famous for its beaches and fish taverns

- Akrotiri – make sure to visit this village as it features an archaeological site, giving you a better look at Santorini's roots. The village also contains a Venetian Castle with an amazing view of the sea and sand below.

- Monolithos – this is actually a beach with several taverns where you can sit down and relax. The beach itself is shallow so you can easily bring the family over and relax knowing that the kids can play safely.

- Megalochori – this traditional village is home of Cycladic churches done in whitewashed colouring

- Vlichada – a small village with its own quiet little beach

Famous For

It stands to reason that Santorini is a favorite for tourists. Ranked as one of the top islands in the world by Travel+Leisure Magazine, the US News, and even the BBC – it's estimated that the island welcomes a total of 2 million tourists on an annual basis.

But what exactly can you find in Santorini that makes it worth visiting?

The sea, sun, and the picturesque view are the primary reasons why people go there. The towns are built in such a way that you can't help but marvel at how vibrant all the shapes and colors are. People who visit Santorini primarily want to kick back and relax, allowing their body to take in the sun and breathe in the smell of the sea. There are also catamaran trips, so tourists can lounge in the middle of the

Aegean Sea for some much-needed unwinding.

Other aspects of Santorini famous with the locals include the thriving Wine Industry and the Architecture.

The Wine Industry is limited but well noted by the wine connoisseurs. There are numerous types of grapes growing in the area, all of which are resistant to diseases – possibly due to the unique soil of the island. Hence, there was no need to replace the vines during the 19th century epidemic – which is probably why these old vines are capable of producing sweet, plump grapes. There are also white wines being produced in the island, known for their citrus and light frankincense aroma. Again, this can be attributed to the unique volcanic soil of the island. While the weather isn't exactly built for wine growing, Santorini wines are respected all over the world and are protected through the Vinsanto and Santorini OPAP designations. Typically, grape yields in the island are only equal to 10 or 20 percent of what is commonly produced in California or France.

The architecture of Santorini is the one thing that will definitely stand out once you visit the island. It's the primary reason why Santorini may be visited all year round. While the sea and wine is seasonal – the architecture looks good no matter what month of the year you decide to visit.

The houses are cubical, made of local stones with their distinctive whitewashed coloring. Set against the hot Greek sun, the resulting imagery is wonderfully striking and unique. In fact, it's easy to recognize Santorini pictures from the architecture alone. The houses built on the precipice of a cliff are small but actually larger inside. Weather-wise, they're perfect because the homes are cool in the summer and warm during the winter.

18

Best Time To Go

Santorini is such a beautiful place with an excellent weather that there's really no "bad time" to visit the island. The fact is that any month will be a good time, but if you want a "great" time, then you'll have to take your personal circumstances into consideration. In this Chapter, we'll talk about the different "purposes" for visiting

Santorini and the months that will serve your purpose best.

If you Want to Avoid All the Tourists – Visit in January to March

January and February are the off-peak seasons – which means that you'll be able to avoid the crush of people in the airport, the bus, the beach, restaurants, and galleries. There are several tourists, but the place will be yours for the most part. Hence, if you hope to take as many solo pictures as possible – this is the best time for it! This also means you'll be paying less for the accommodation as hotels do their best to get in more people during the off-peak season.

The downside is that many of the shops or hotels won't be open as some of them operate only during the high-tourist season. You might also find it harder to visit famous coffee shops and restaurants because they may not be operating.

Come March, the number of tourists will significantly increase – but not so much that you'll have to worry about the crowd. During this time, there should only be 20% of the average tourist numbers during peak season. Hence, the hotels will still have sufficient slots with prices that are relatively cheaper than the peak months.

If the Crowd Spurs You On – Visit from April to October

These are the peak season months with the crowd density anywhere from 70% to 100% with the ultimate peak happening on the months of July and August. Hence, if you're not really a fan of crowds but still want to enjoy all the tourist attractions, you should choose either May or October where the tourist percentage is around 70% only. The upside is that all the tourist attractions will be open. Restaurants will have their doors wide open and coffee shops will offer all their best delicacies. Shops will be packed with souvenir items and so on.

The downside is of course, the prices will be a little higher compared to the off-peak season. You'll also have a harder time booking a hotel because despite the amount of hotels in Santorini, the number of tourists is even more compelling. If your Santorini vacations fall under any of these months, then make sure you've got advanced booking on a hotel – otherwise you might find yourself spending more for a room for the night.

If You Want Warm Weather and Lounging on the Beach

If you're visiting Santorini for the white sandy beaches, the best months to go would be anywhere from June to September. Incidentally, this also falls within the peak season because a lot of people want the warm weather of this beautiful island. Should that stop you? Of course not! If you plan your holiday right, a peak-season visit shouldn't be a problem. From June to September, the beaches are open, and you can happily swim on the sea and wear summer dresses all day. Before or after these months, the cold season kicks in and the swimming is no longer a good idea. You can still chill out on the beach if you want – but you might want to put on several layers to help with the cold.

If You Want a Packaged Tour

Tours are often offered depending on the best time for their availability. The contents of the packaged tours vary depending on the travel agency that offers them. For the most part though, the tours are any of the following:

- Sunset Sailing Cruise in Caldera
- Luxury Catamaran Day Cruise
- Santorini Sunset Wine Tour
- Santorini Private Tour
- Santorini Photography Tour

These are often offered during the peak season from the late par of May up to the early days of October. The Wine Tour and the Photography Tour can be availed up to November but in truth, the island as so many photo-worthy places that you can walk around and find a subject every few minutes.

If You Want to go Sightseeing

Sightseeing doesn't necessarily require warm weather. You just want a pleasant weather that allows you to walk around and take in all the beauty of this island. If this is your goal in Santorini, then the months of March, April, May, October, and November would be perfect. It's not too cold to walk around in your best comfortable clothes although you might want to pack some items in anticipation of a slight drizzle.

So let's break this down on a monthly basis. Here's what you can expect when visiting Santorin depending on the month.

January

- Tourist: January is an off-peak season month so there will be fewer tourists
- Weather: Still a little cold, you wouldn't want to go sunbathing at this time.

February

- Tourist: Another off-peak season, you can expect to have most of Santorini all to yourself
- Weather: Still cold, but you can opt for sightseeing and photography tours

March

- Tourist: During the latter part of March, you should be able to notice a slight increase in the number of tourists
- Weather: The weather is set to get warm starting from this month, but it's still not a good idea for swimming

April

- Tourist: By April, there will be a sharp increase in the amount of people in the island.
- Weather: Still cold but definitely better than the previous months of the year.

May

- Tourist: Tourist numbers should reach around 70% of the maximum at this point.
- Weather: The weather starts to become warmer and the beach begins to open up to visitors.

June

- Tourist: With the warm weather a certainty, you'll find that the number of tourists will remain extensive.
- Weather: Warm weather. You can visit the beach at this point.

July

- Tourist: Still packed, the island will start to liven up with all the tourists streaming in from all over the world.
- Weather: Wonderfully warm, you can lounge on the beach and do some sunbathing.

August

- Tourist: This is the ultimate peak month – which means that the number of people can be anywhere from 100 to 110 percent.
- Weather: The warmest point of this island, August gives you the chance to enjoy everything on the island.

September

- Tourist: Another peak season. Make sure to book your rooms and restaurants as early as possible.
- Weather: Warm weather makes for perfect boat tours.

October to December

- Tourist: Everything winds down at this point. The tourist numbers are starting to go down as the weather turns colder.
- Weather: While boat tours and lounging on the beach aren't good options anymore – you'll find that there are lots more you can do in the island.

19

Safety Tips

Santorini is a relatively safe city with few pickpockets or snatchers who might get your valuables as you stroll around the city. Typical safety measures such as having your passport kept in a vault are recommended during your stay here. Weather-wise however, here's what you should keep in mind:

- Always put on sunscreen, especially during the summer months of

Santorini. While the hot weather is one of the reasons why people visit the island, very few really appreciate the impact of the hot, Greek sun. A bottle of SPF30 sun screen should always be in your bag. This should cost around 20 Euro.

- Bring a hat and shades for protection all the time. Your sun block will provide for several hours of protection, depending on its SPF.
- The cliffs and low walls can be quite tempting to children but can cause danger, especially with the steps. The same problem may be present for elderly tourists so it's best to skip these areas unless you're absolutely sure of the save.
- Cave exploration is also a wonderful activity in Santorini. Note though that all caves come with a predetermined path that should be followed at ALL times. Deviating from the path can lead you to unstable grounds, thereby causing an accident.
- Stray dogs are quite common in Santorini. Although many of them are friendly, there are those that can be hostile – especially when it comes to food. Don't be alarmed if these dogs decide to follow you around – especially during a hiking trail. They've been known to do that, often trailing people from one village to the next.

20

Transport

If you're coming in from other countries, then you should know that Santorini only has one international airport known as the Santorini Thira Airport located north of the Kamari Village. It currently accommodates Olympic Air, Aegean Airlines, and Ryanair as well as chartered and scheduled flights.

It is estimated that the airport handles roughly 2 million passengers every year.

So you have several options for reaching Santorini which includes the following:

- Any Country to Athens to Santorini by Plane or Ferry
- Any Country to Thessaloniki to Santorini by Plane or Ferry
- Direct International Flight to Santorini

Any Country to Any Part of Greece

There are two popular landing spots in Greece that you can use as a main jump off point to Santorini. This is Athens and Thessaloniki. Both have state of the art, international airports the offer connecting flights to the island.

From Any Part of Greece to Santorini by Plane

You'll find that there are several possible jump off points from Greece that could help you get to Santorini. Athens is perhaps the most common jump off point because it has lots of incoming international flights on a daily basis. Here's what you should know about the trip:

- Athens to Santorini by Plane – the trip would take about 50 minutes through multiple airlines. Considering the fact that Santorini is a popular destination, this means you can choose from any of the 29 or more flights to the island on a daily basis. The receiving airport is the JTR Airport as already mentioned above.
- Thessaloniki to Santorini by Plane – the flight from this jump off point is a bit longer – but not by much. The actual flight should take 1 hour and 5 minutes. Unfortunately, flights from Thessaloniki to Santorini is limited, averaging at just 4 each day, typically through Ellinair 18 Airlines.

Reaching Santorini by Ferry

- Athens to Santorini by Ferry–the ferry trip would definitely take longer but on the plus side, you can probably enjoy the sea more in this situation. There are two ports in Athens that you can use: Pireaus or Rafina. You can take a bus or taxi from the Athens airport to the port. From there, you can buy a ticket from any of the three ferry services going to Santorini. The ferry trip could be anywhere from 5 hours to 9 hours, depending on the ferry you're taking.
- Thessaloniki to Santorini by Ferry

Public Transportation in Santorini

- Renting a Car – if you want to explore Santorini at your own pace and you're brave enough to do the driving, then you can hire a car directly from the airport. There are actually three companies that offer hire cars and you can book them online even before landing on the island.
- Private Transfer – of course, there's also the possibility that your hotel booking already includes a private transfer that will wait for you at the airport. If this is the case, then you should have any problem reaching your hotel.
- Taxi Service – a taxi service would be perfect not just for transfer to the hotel but also for your everyday excursions in the city. Note though that taxi services often have a value of more than €20, depending on where you intend to go.
- Bus Transport – you can also make use of bus transportation if you're part of a large group. You also have the option of using the public transportation – again by bus.
- Public Transportation – this is the only mode of public transport in Santorini and is being operated by the KTEL Company. The cost

of the fare from the Santorini airport to the main center should be around €2. Since there's only one terminal, you shouldn't have a hard time finding a bus.

Keep note of the following however:

1. You cannot book or purchase a ticket online. You'll have to be there and ready to take the trip in order to get a ticket.

2. Keep in mind that drivers only take cash. They accept EUR currency.

3. On weekdays, you can catch any of the 4 scheduled journeys, the last one leaving as early as 15:10 from the airport. On the weekends however, there are only 3 journeys on the city center, the last one leaving at 15:40 from the airport.

4. Note that the bus does not run at night or during the afternoon. Fortunately, you can still take a taxi or hire a private car to get around the city.

5. The bus route is: Santorini Airport – Karterados – Messaria – Fira Bus Station.

Phone:+30 22860 25404

ATV and Bike Rental

Renting ATVs and bikes deserve special attention here because while they are definitely many of those in Santorini, not all are worth having. Specifically, some rental agencies will talk you into getting old and broken down ATVs or bikes that will likely make it harder for you to move around the city. This is recognized as a scam among the tourists and is best avoided.

Of course, that doesn't mean there's no worthwhile rental agencies in the island. Make a point of reserving only with a reputable ATV company – ideally those with brand-new looking vehicles. Inspect the vehicle first before signing any contract.

Phone:+30 2286 082833 (Bike Rental)

21

Top 5 Affordable Hotels

Santorini derives much of its income from tourism – which is why the island is full of hotels – each one offering an amazing view of the city and the waters. Here are the best hotels in the island according to visitors.

Amber Lights Villas

This 4-star hotel can be found on the Eastern portion of the island. It's less than a mile away from the village of Imerovigli which makes walking around the town easier. Rooms open up to a view of the Aegean Sea with a terrace that whets the appetite every morning.

All rooms are air-conditioned, but you probably won't need them thanks to the refreshing air from the sea. Amenities of the hotel include wireless internet, a hot tub, a private pool, space center, hammam, access to a garden, restaurants, and an on-site bar. Depending on the room you get, you'll have an in-room mini bar, a flat screen, an iPad, a coffee machine and 1 or 2 separate bedrooms. If you're thinking about hiring a private car, then the hotel has more than enough room for free private parking.

All in all, it's a favorite for couples and trips for groups of friends. It's only 3.7 miles away from the Thira Airport with staff that speak both Greek and English.

Phone: +30 2286 036269

Beldevere Hotel

Located at Fira, this hotel offers a magnificent view of the Aegean Sea as well as the caldera of a volcano. Definitely something worth seeing on a daily basis, Beldevere Hotel amps up the experience by giving you the kind room with handcrafted furnishings and traditional furniture. It really sets off the Santorini experience with the added benefit of being walking distance to museums, shops, and the nightlife. Close by is the Villa of Oia and Akrotiri – both of which are frequented due to the amazing views and the even more amazing sunset. There's also the Minoan Town known for being preserved in volcanic ash. This town is actually 3,500 years old!

Additional amenities include living rooms in junior suites and an amazing rain shower found in all units. There's also an outdoor pool, a gym, a bar, and even a 24-hour reception and concierge service. The staff speaks English so requesting anything should not be a problem.

Phone: +30 2286 025650

Cori Rigas Suites

Located on the Fira Cliffs, the Cori Rigas Suites actually offer a series of condos with a view of the Santorini Volcano and the Aegena Sea. While you can definitely enjoy the sea water – weather permitting – you are always welcome to try out their outdoor pool for a quick dip. There are two types of rooms depending on the view: one gives you a look at the Volcano while the other one opens up to a courtyard or a shared terrace looking into the sea. Either option is good and gives you one amazing view from the moment you open your eyes.

The hotel itself is packed with amenities including wireless internet and made-to-order breakfast. You also have the option of getting a massage and anything else you want that's offered through their full-service spa. Staff speaks several languages including Russian, Greek, German, and English. While the hotel is popular with couples, it actually accepts family bookings and even has babysitting services at an additional charge.

Phone: +30 2286 025251

Kalisti Hotel and Suites

Location: Fira, Fira

If you're looking for a combination of the night life and rest, then look no further than the Kalisti Hotel. It's smack in the middle of Fira Town, literally just yards away from the Caldera. Thanks to its ideal location, the hotel managed to set up a sun-lounger terrace and an outdoor hot tub. You can also check out their pool.

They offer a breakfast buffet so you can fill yourself up before spending the rest of the day exploring Santorini.

Facilities include television, wireless internet, and even babysitting services for family groups. Bathrooms come with luxurious toiletries, slippers, and hairdryer. Each room also comes with a standard mini-bar. There's also a pool bar nearby that serves food and drinks all through the day.

Of course, the proximity of Fira Town means that you have the whole village to explore so there's really no need to hang around the hotel itself. There's a whole world to explore outdoors, especially with the taxis and buses only 50 meters away. Families can take advantage of the babysitting services while they book one of the many tours offered like walking tours, horseback riding, diving, hiking, bike tours, canoeing, fishing, and other as weather permits.

Languages spoken by the staff include Italian, French, Spanish, English, Greek, and German.

+30 2286 022317

Modernity Suites

Location: Fira

A favourite in the town of Fira, this particular hotel rests on top of the Caldera, giving you a view unlike any other. The suites are elegant, some of which come with outdoor hot tubs – perfect for couple vacations. This makes it one of the few hotels that's still perfect even if you're visiting during the cold season. To top it off, you'll enjoy a view of the Aegean Sea and the volcano from your balcony – all while luxuriating in the modern amenities the hotel has to offer.

The suites come with built-in sofas, arched walls, a mini-bar, kettle services, built in shower, and a tablet. There's also daily breakfast served directly to your private terrace. If you feel like nibbling on something, there's a snack menu available the whole day. Suffice it to say, Modernity Suites is built to make sure your every whim is met during your vacation.

Staff speak English and Greek.

Phone: +30 2286 036411

Hotel Matina
Location: Kamari Beach, Santorini

Aside from the stunning view of the beach from this hotel, you're given the added benefit of being literally 3 minutes away from the Kamari Beach. Every time you open your hotel room, you'll be greeted by a breath of fresh salt air, whether you decide to go during the cold or the warm season. On the flipside is a garden that you can enjoy regardless of the weather.

The hotel itself hosts a swimming pool and a pool-side bar. There's also a snack bar and for those who want to fill their days with activities, you can book yourself a snorkelling, cycling, hiking, windsurfing, or cycling activity through the hotel itself. Or you can just start in your room and watch television or scroll through your feed through their wireless internet. A family-run hotel, the Hotel Matina is extensive enough that the staff accommodates four languages: Italian, English, Greek, and French.

An added bonus for this hotel is that it's pet friendly! Guests are allowed to bring their pets upon advance notice with no additional charges.

Phone: +30 2286 031491

Hotel Star Santorini
Location: Megalochori

Just 50 minutes away from the caldera, the Hotel is situated in the traditional settlement of Megalochori. All rooms come with balconies that offer an amazing view of the sea or if you prefer, a look at the lush garden beautifully maintained by the hotel staff. The rooms come with cable TV, radio, hairdryer, and a small fridge.

The beauty of Hotel Star is in its simplicity, giving you just enough facilities for a comfortable stay without overwhelming you with too many options. This gives you the chance to really sink into the experience and focus on what you really want to do during your Santorini trip.

After sunning yourself at the Perissa Beach which is around 1.91 miles away – you can come back to the fresh water pool and the poolside snack bar. Couples will also love the hot tub in the hotel and upload their favourite pictures through the hotel-wide wireless internet. For families, there's a playground for the younger guests. Wake up every day to a large spread of a breakfast buffet spread out in the hotel's breakfast room.

If you want to explore the town of Fira, the centre is just 3.7 miles away from the hotel. You can also indulge your inner history buff with a trip to
Acrotiri which is just 1.21 miles away.

Phone: +30 2286 081198

Sea Side Beach Hotel
Location: Kamari

Just one minute away from the Kamari Beach, the Sea Side Beach Hotel is aptly named. Despite being literally a stone's throw away from the beach, the hotel comes with an outdoor pool and a hot tub. Built pursuant to the local architecture, the hotel is a beauty in itself with a decidedly modern interior packed with air conditioned rooms and free wireless internet.

The hotel offers a breakfast buffet to get your day started the right way. From the restaurant or even your own hotel room, you can enjoy the sea view while savouring the sumptuous dishes on offer. There's also an on-site tavern that provides local Greek dishes. If you just prefer to laze around with aromatic coffee, there's a coffee shop on-site too.

Through the hotel, you can book several activities including water sports, diving off-site, hiking off-site, canoeing, and snorkelling. You can also have the hotel arrange a car rental to take you to the centre of Fira for a much-needed nightlife with the locals or some shopping.

The staff is trained to speak English, Greek, and Italian so you can always communicate exactly what you want.

Phone: +30 2286 033403

22

Top Rated Restaurants And Coffee Shops

Top Rated Restaurants in Santorini

Selene Restaurant, Pygros

Originally established in Fira, this Michelin Star Restaurant recently moved to Pygros and managed to maintain its exquisite food all the way. The new location definitely added to the ambience as the restaurant offers a terrific view of the sprawling city, mountains, and the horizon. It's the perfect place for a romantic dinner – or lunch if you're in the mood for it.

Ranked as one of the best restaurants in Santorini, Selene is known for their tasteful servings of Greek cuisine. If you really want to make the most out of your Santorini experience, then you should definitely try out signature dishes offered from this restaurant which includes any of the following:

- Suckling Pig – a small portion of pork cooked with potato foam and served with potato peel chips. The pig is thickened with wine, brawn, pita bread, baked onion, tomato jam, and garlic butter.
- Lamb with Trahana – the lamb is cooked with liver, butter of Greek coffee, and powdered porcini. The cream of sour Trahana adds to the overall flavour and gives it the tender lamb meat a distinctive taste.
- Quail – legs of quail is served with pureed carrots, gelee of beer, poached apple, ketchup, and red Florina peppers
- Spanakorizo – Selene managed to add a twist to this classical cuisine. Typically, Spanakorizo is a combination of spinach, onions, dill, lemon, and rice. However, the restaurant adds leeks, kale, yogurt, sheep's milk, and red-raspberry.
- Octopus Yiouvetsi – made with handmade orzo, grilled octopus, olive pate, truffles, and mushroom chips.

Phone:+30 2286 022249

Nikolas Taverna

Located in Fira, the Nikolas Taverna also goes by the name of "The Cave of Nikolas". They opened up in 1967 and continues to operate until today. They're quite a big hit with the tourists with locals only visiting the restaurant only when they know it's not packed with people. Close to the sea, the Nikolas Tavera offers homemade meals with ingredients that come directly from the family farm – how much closer can you get to natural with that?

This is actually the older tavern in the island – which makes it very easy to find. No need to whip out your smartphone – you can ask any local and they'd point you to the right direction. Due to the high demand however, you'd want to make a reservation – especially if you're visiting during the peak months. The good news is that online reservations are welcomed.

Some of the food items on offer include but are not limited to the following:

- Old Time Moussaka – this is the restaurant's most famous dish, providing you with the chance to sample the entire island in a single plate. The product contains fresh ingredients of eggplant, potato, zucchini, chloro cheese, pepper, mzithra, tomato sauce, basil, and minit.
- Lamb Stew in the Pot – tender lamb mixed with organically grown vegetables.
- Fava Risotto with Seafood – combined with seafood and rice

Phone: +30 2286 082303

Kapari Wine Restaurant

A restaurant with the kind of view made for Instagram, the Kapari

Wine Restaurant offers not just a gastronomical experience but also access to some of the best wines available in the island. Quick and easy to find thanks to its accessible location, you shouldn't have any problem hiring a private car to take you to the location. Google Maps should also be very helpful at this point and if you're anywhere within the town, you might be able to walk your way to the restaurant.

Kapari Wine is primarily famous for its black risotto, cheese pie, chocolate mousse, and lamb. Note that Kapari Wine Restaurant forms part of the Kapari Natural Resort which also makes for a great hotel to stay in. Just make sure to watch out during the peak season because this restaurant can be quite packed.

Phone: +30 2286 021120

Pitogyros

Located at Oia, the restaurant isn't exactly a restaurant. Don't expect all the bells and whistles in this restaurant because Pitogyros is a grill place packed with genuine Greek street food. It's as authentic as you can get to Santorini's flavours without having a full blooded local cooking for you in a family setting. The restaurant itself is fairly small – which is why you'll need to get there as early as possible to get the few stands available.

The reward though is amazing as Pitogyros is considered to have the best gyros and souvlakia in Santorini. If you feel like there's not enough room for you, then just take out some of the food and bring them to your hotel. There's no reservation here as the grill house is as casual as it gets. It might take some waiting time during the peak season, but if you show up – then you'll surely be fed.

Phone: +30 2286 071119

Koukoumavlos

Another favourite in the area, Koukoumavlos rated well in tripadvisor – and for a very good reason! Their signature dishes include the carpaccio and scampi with spiced apple, white chocolate sauce, and caviar. The restaurant is famous for offering traditional Greek dishes with a twist – while at the same time giving guests the option for something more familiar.

Phone: +30 2286 023807

Katharos Lounge

Another cool restaurant to visit with multiple vegetarian options, the Katharos Lounge isn't exactly close to the sea and horizon. In fact, there's very little to see from their current location. Of course, if you visit during an opportune time, you'd find that the location can be quite compelling and stress-relieving. But what makes this a popular one in Santorini? It's one of the few restaurants with a menu for vegetarians. If you're a vegan or just want to make sure you stay in shape during your vacation, then the Katharos Lounge would be a good bet.

Phone: +30 697 096 6754

Top Rated Coffee Shops

Coffee Island

Arguably one of the best coffee shops in Santorini, Coffee Island is a favourite not just by the tourists but also by the locals. Located at Agios Athanasios Thiras, the coffee shop is popular enough that you can reach it by asking around the locals. You can also ask your hotel's front desk for directions or really – just use Google Maps because the area is wonderfully indicated through Google.

They serve all kinds of coffee from hot to cold, espresso, Greek coffee, iced tea, and hot tea. They also offer packed coffee beans so if you ever find one that you love, you can easily buy a pack and take a bit of Santorini home with you. While the coffee shop doesn't accept online orders, you can easily check their website and pick a favourite even before you enter their store.

Phone: +30 2286 036330

218 Café

Located in Oia, the 218 Café is popular for its rooftop location that makes coffee drinking a pleasurable experience. This isn't like your local Starbucks where you can grab and run coffee. No, every sip here is an experience in itself as you enjoy the setting sun over the horizon. Perched right on the rim of the caldera, it's one of the best places to end the day after a hectic time at the beach.

Phone: +30 2286 071801

Mylos Café

Located at Firostefani, the café has the unique feature of being built around a windmill. In fact, the word Mylos means windmill and thus, so high up that you can easily see a vast view of the Santorini waters. The café is set up in such a way that you can comfortably rest your back against the pillows and sip coffee – whether hot or cold, strong or creamy. It can be quite crowded during the high season so you'll have to get there pretty early if you want the best seats.

Phone: +30 2286 025640

Skiza Café

Situated in Oia, it's not surprising that Skiza is famous with the locals and tourists. This isn't just a café but also functions as a cafeteria, displaying excellent pastries freshly baked on a daily basis. There are two floors comprising Skiza with the patio being a particular favourite for many. Go here during the late afternoon and you'll be treated to a stunning view of the sun and sea – complete with the cool breeze, compliments of the high altitude of the café building.

Phone: +30 2286 071569

Francos

Located at Pyrgos, the café is also situated near the cliff, thereby giving you a stunning view of the sunset. The café itself is excellent, built primarily for those who want to sit back and enjoy their coffee. A lounge café, Francos serves all kinds of drinks done in the traditional Greek way or if you prefer something a little creamier, they have those too!

Phone :+30 2286 033957

23

Top Museums And Art Galleries

Top Museums

Megaro Gyzi Museum

Founded in 1980, this museum is home to relics and depict the cultural background of Thira. This was originally a family mansion during the 17th century and was able to survive major damage during the 1965 earthquake. Inside you'll find authentic engravings, paintings of Santorini, old photos, and historical manuscripts.

Phone: +30 2286 023077

Wine Museum

If you can't go on a Wine Tour, you might as well visit the Wine Museum featuring the history and life of wine as far back as 1660. The museum is quite unique in that it is situated inside a cave, keeping the temperature cool even during the warm season.

Phone: +30 2286 031322

Lignos Folklore Museum

Built in 1861, the museum was an old winery that's a combination of wine memorabilia, artworks, manuscripts, books, and even a cavern that shows exactly how the volcanic eruption affected the ground.

Phone:+30 2286 022792

Museum of Minerals and Fossils

Offering numerous displays of minerals and fossils, this Museum in Perissa has garnered global attention due to its unique displays. The museum puts emphasis on how the island of Santorini is connected to the world by virtue of old fossils and animals found in its landscape.

Phone:+30 697 640 3771

Naval Maritime Museum

A restored mansion of the 19th century, the museum focuses on the navy and what the Thirans did to contribute to the war time defence of Greece. If you're a fan of various equipment, you'll find here sailing vessels, photographs, models, and Thiran ships.

Phone:+30 2286 071156

Best Galleries

Art Space

A combination of art plus wine making, Art Space is a quick stop but comprehensive – especially with the right guide. In here, you can buy bottles of wine even as you appreciate the age-old method of wine making. This was one of the few first wine producers in the island.

Phone: +30 693 289 9509

Oia Treasures of Art Gallery

Offering a massive array of Greek contemporary art, it's tough not to appreciate the bold colours on display in this gallery. The exhibits are intact but pleasing to the senses – a quiet place to be if you want to bring back the balance during your trip. If you go during the off-peak season, there's also a good chance you'll have the place all to yourself.

Phone:+30 2286 072148

Art of the Loom

Containing oil paintings, ceramics, jewellery, glass, and bronze items – the Art of the Loom Museum is a study of beauty in every corner. In fact, the building itself is a work of art, originally intended as a winery in 1866. The spot managed to retain its structural integrity after that 1956 earthquake and was renovated only in 2010 into its current condition.

Phone: +30 2286 021617

MATI Art Gallery

MATI primarily exhibits the work of a single artist: Yorgos Kypris. He's a sculptor known worldwide for his work on human behaviour and managing to mould them into artistic expressions. Despite the fact that all the items on display only come from one artist, there's no question that the range of creations is mind blowing.

Phone: +30 2286 023814

Mnemossyne Gallery

Imagine the whitewashed exterior of Oia buildings but indoors. This is what the gallery looks like as it opens its doors to visitors all year round. This is the place you want to be in if you want to find a bundle of local artwork by local artists. From jewellery to fine art photographs – the gallery gives you an added appreciation for beauty. It also has an idyllic location because it's only a stone's throw away from the sunset spot of Oia.

Phone: +30 2286 072142

24

Top Bars And Night Clubs

The island may seem like an introvert's dream during the day, but the Santorini social life is actually packed – especially come night time. Following are the top bars and night clubs in the area:

Top Bars

Tranquilo Beach Bar

Location: Perissa Beach

Perfect for chilling out, this beach bar is a favourite among singles and couples alike. They offer cocktails as well as veggies to keep partying all night without worrying about the extra calories. Perhaps their best event is the Latin party where you can dance the salsa from sunset to sunrise.

+30 2286 085230

Wet Stories Beach Bar

Location: Perivolos Beach

With lounge chairs, sunbeds, and giant bean bags, you'll find this beach bar the ideal location for a group's night out. They serve fancy cocktails as well as beer and offer mainstream music all through the night. This makes the spot perfect for fun conversations with your friends. They offer beach volleyball facilities – so you can burn off the alcohol even as you get drunk.

+30 2286 082990

Theros Wave Beach Bar
Location: Vlychada Beach

This one's not as packed as the rest – and that's actually the best part. This is because the Theros Wave Beach Bar was built for couples – hence the ultra-romantic setting. In case you don't know, this beach is also known alternatively as the White Beach. While it's primarily a bar, they also serve exquisite food – perfect for honeymooners.

+30 2286 112015

Casablanca Lounge Cocktail Bar
Location: Fira

While beach bars are fun, you should also check out the bars offshore. They host excellent parties with the whole shebang of DJs playing funk and soul music. This cocktail bar is perfect for all kinds of visitors, whether single, couples, or groups. Due to the fact that it's located at Fira, the floor is always packed – especially in August.

+30 2286 027188

Two Brothers

Location: Fira

Dubbed as a party bar, this is the place you want to be if you love to get up and dance. The place has shisha set up all over the place – allowing you to chill, drink, and dance in that order. Ideal for singles who want to meet someone during their summer in Santorini, the dance floor and music is constantly encouraging you to let loose.

Phone: +30 2286 023061

Top Night Clubs

Enigma Club

A pillar of Santorini's nightlife, Enigma has been around for as long as Santorini has been a favourite. Inside, you can dance your heart out or you can choose to sit in the small balcony and just savour the night air. Either way, you're going to get a slice of the unique Santorini taste.

Phone: +30 2286 022466

Koo Club

When it comes to most popular club in Santorini, there are really only two names competing for the top spot: that's Enigma Club and the Koo Club. If you want to experience night life in the island, you have to hit at least one of these Clubs. Koo Club has an indoor room and an outdoor spot for dancers – three bars dotting the place to keep you filled up with drinks.

Phone:+30 2286 022025

Night Flight

Found at Avis Beach in Kamari, the Night Flight Club opened only in 2015 but is already a popular spot – especially for the locals. Set by the beach, you have the option of socializing indoors or taking a romantic walk by the shore. They serve cocktails and food in a completely casual atmosphere.

Phone: +30 2286 032034

Town Club

Located in Thira, the Town Club is a favourite for the younger visitors of Santorini – as well as the younger locals. The Club hosts events practically on a nightly basis – which means that there's always something new when you drop by.

Phone: +30 2286 023675

Mamounia Club

Hey, if you're looking for traditional Greek music to dance to – then this is the place you want to be. Despite the local music however, the club itself is designed in ultra-modern glasswork with bright coloured palm tree designs that throws an amazing shade all over the place.

Phone: +30 698 297 0799

25

Top Famous Landmarks

In the interest of keeping your options fresh and open, this Chapter will talk about the top landmarks in Santorini without taking in consideration the other places that's already been mentioned. What does this mean? Well, for example – we've already talked about the Selene Restaurant in the later Chapter and while Selene is definitely a Santorini landmark, we're not going to discuss it here to avoid repetition.

So aside from the top bars, clubs, museums, galleries, and restaurants previously discussed – what other landmarks does Santorini have that bears remembering?

Here are the top 5 that every local should know:

Profitis Ilias

This is official Santorini's highest peak – which means that you'll be getting the best vantage point of the sunset or sunrise from this area. The Mt. Profitis Ilias is measures at 584 meters and at the peak, you'll find that Profitis Ilias Monastery. It's open to the public so you can walk in and marvel at the brilliance of architecture and the difficulty of opening such a building on the top peak. Fun fact: the monastery was a site for one of the many secret schools that ran during the Turkish period.

Ancient Thira

Ancient Thira dates back as early as the ninth century BC and is home to Hellenistic Temples.

They're already in ruins, but that shouldn't stop you from being able to appreciate the landscape that's littered with stone structures. Imagine – hundreds of years ago, these were dwellings where ancient people lived, walked, and breathed.

There's nothing quite like feeling an attachment to the past by touching the same stones children probably drew on during the 9th century.

Caldera

The caldera is in itself a landmark of Santorini – although in reality, the caldera defines the city. It's basically a depression which resulted from the volcanic eruption. The size of the caldera gives you a fairly good idea of how big the volcano was – and how powerfully it erupted at the time.

It ranks as one of the top landmarks in the world and you don't have to pay anything to get there. The spot is open to the public for free at all times – and if you have a hotel in Oia, then you're basically next door neighbours with the caldera!

Lighthouse

Found in Akrotiri, the lighthouse is a coastal tower that's been the subject of one too many photographs. It can be because of the whitewashed walls, the striking tower on top, or the fact that no one's ever been inside – but the tower is a strong highlight of any Santorini visit. Why can't you go inside? The lighthouse is operational and under the control of the Greek Navy, which only adds to its attraction.

Old Port

Every local knows where the Old Port is and can easily lead you to the location. With the cable car, you can reach this landmark quickly which can also be a jump off point to other landmarks of Santorini.

While still in use, the Old Port has a very traditional feel to it and with the addition of several shops along the way, you can buy the odd knick knacks for people at home.

26

Things You Can Only Do In Santorini

When visiting a new place, you'd always want to do something that's completely unique in that area. That way, you can always have a unique memory for your vacation. So what exactly is unique in Santorini? Here are the top 5 activities that should tell you exactly what you want to include in your itinerary:

Swim in the Red Beach

Since the Red Beach was already discussed in previous Chapters, it only bears repeating that the Red Beach is an experience you can only have in the island.

Most beaches are done in white sand – but the Red Beach will offer you a wide range of colours in red and rose. It's a unique setup due to the remnants of the volcanic eruption on the island.

Oia Village Visit

When you see pictures of Santorini with the whitewashed buildings and vibrant blue tops – you're seeing an image of the Oia Village.

Know that: (1) there's no other place like it in Greece and (2) the reality of the villages are more amazing than they appear on the photos.

Take your time and stroll through the place, all the while taking pictures. Maybe wear something dark or blue to add some startling contrasts to your pictures.

Local Fava Beans

They say half of the reason people travel is for the food – which is why you should definitely taste dishes that are uniquely served in the area. The local fava beans fit this need to a T.

Akrotiri Archeological Site

Learn a little bit of history while you travel through this archaeological site. Again, this has been discussed in a previous Chapter so the mention of the site is really just a reminder of what you should aim for during your Santorini vacation.

+30 2286 081939

The Amazing Sunset

It might sound unfair to include sunsets in this list considering how every sunset is unique. However, there's something quite breathtaking about the Santorini sunset.

Maybe it's because when viewing the sunset, you're basically on top of a cliff – giving you a better vantage point as opposed to viewing it from below. Either way, you should definitely leave some time during dusk to just sit back and take in the setting horizon.

Shopping at Epilekton

Found at Oia's Central Square, it's tough to visit Santorini without bringing a little bit of it back with you. This can be done through Epilekton which offers a wide range of art pieces and handicrafts. The Central Square itself is a miasma of shopping finds, giving you the chance to jump from one spot to the next as you inspect possible souvenirs for your trip. Keep your valuables close though – while Santorini is relatively safe – you'd want to make sure you're not losing anything valuable.

Phone: +30 2286 071686

27

3-Day itinerary

With so much things to do and places to see in Santorini, the amount of time you spend may not be enough to fully explore the island. This is why it's a good idea to plan your trip ahead of time so you can hit the highlights of the island and come home with unique memories of this beautiful Greek place. In this Chapter, we'll talk about your ideal 3-day itinerary for Santorini and which places and what activities are best done during your time there.

Day 1

On Day 1, we're going to assume that you arrived in Santorini during the morning and will therefore start exploring in the afternoon. That should give you more than enough time to rest and relax before checking out this wonderful island. So what do you do on your first day? Now, keep in mind that your tour will largely depend on the location of your hotel or which village you're staying in. Fortunately, Santorini is small enough that you can actually go from one village to the next without too much lost time.

Wine Tour

This is perhaps the best thing you can do during your first day.

Santorini's wine has won awards and unlike anything else in the world. At the same time, the wine should help you relax after that gruelling trip from Athens to Santorini.

The wine tour usually covers up half the day so you can actually choose this to kick off your Santorini vacation. The wine tour lets you see the wine making process from the ground up. The beauty of this wine tour is that it picks you up from your hotel and then drops you off again – which means that you don't have to worry about transportation on your very first day. You can go exploring on foot if you want to on the next day.

The drop off is equally important because no wine tour is complete without wine tasting. You'll be taken to 3 different wineries in the island and treated to a total of 12 wine styles together with salami, olives, and chees. By the end of the wine tour, you'll be completely relaxed and ready to have your dinner, watch the sunset, and settle in for a full night's sleep.

Tel/fax +30 22860 28358 (wine tour)
   Mob. + 30 6937 084958

E-mail: info@santoriniwinetour.com

Santorini Sunset

In all honesty, every sunset on Santorini is a sunset worth watching. Thanks to the unique positioning of the island, there's literally no town where the sunset can be termed as bad. Pick your spot and just enjoy the sunset on your first night in Santorini.

Day 2

On your second day, you have the full 24 hours to play with so there are more chances of controlling your schedule. Here are some of the top places to visit while in Santorini:

Experience Greek Coffee

There's nothing quite the smell of fresh coffee in the morning. While you may choose to taste Greek Coffee in your hotel or opt to visit one of the many coffee shops in the area, Greek Coffee is something you definitely don't want to miss. Make a point of visiting a coffee shop at any point of the day. You're on vacation – coffee shouldn't be limited in the morning!

Red Beach

The Red Beach is the most popular beach destination in Santorini, so it makes sense to check it out. The name is aptly made because the sand is coloured red. The number of people on the Red Beach may vary, depending on whether its peak season or not. Even if you choose not to take a dip however, witnessing the beach itself can already be a big achievement. There's a few beaches in the world with this kind of setup.

Black Beach

Santorini is also known for the Black Beach which – as the name suggests – is covered by a layer of black sand. These come from the volcanic eruption in the past and makes for a striking image in your Instagram. Feel free to take a dip, depending on the weather.

Sunset Boat Tour

Of course, you can also choose to watch the sunset while on a boat. In fact, you shouldn't miss this unique experience. Santorini is famous for its beach and its sunset – the boat tour gives you the best of both worlds in one go. Dinner usually comes with the boat tour, whetting your appetite with the strong smell of salt and sea.

Archaeological Exploration

The problem with a beach exploration is that you can only do it during the warmer weather. If you visit Santorini during the colder climate, you still have other options such as the archaeological tour in Akrotiri. You can go there even without a guide and explore remnants of an ancient civilization at your own leisure. Believe it or not, the remnants here are older than Pompeii but the beauty of the items remain intact. There are guides available as well if you want to appreciate the story behind the relics.

Check out the Local Cuisine

Obviously, you'll visit more than one of the many restaurants discussed above for your meals. Whatever happens, don't forget to visit local eateries or those that serve street food because you don't want to much Santorini in its most authentic flavour.

Souvenir Shopping

Of course, don't forget to do some souvenir shopping around the latter part of the day. Shopping is best done during the first or second day because this gives you the chance to properly pack your stuff.

Day 3

Your itinerary for your third and last day on Santorini would depend largely on when you'd actually leave the island. Ideally, your trip out is early the next morning – which gives you another full day to explore the island. If this isn't the case however, you'd want to pack as much fun in the few hours you have left before you leave for the airport or the ferry.

So what should you do on your third day?

Fira-Oia Hike

There's nothing quite like a relaxing walk from Fira to Oia and then back again, allowing you to explore the caldera along the way. Remember that the caldera is the defining aspect of Santorini so it would be a shame if you couldn't take it all in – especially on your last day. The walk can be quite peaceful.

Photography Tour

If you're not really a fan of a hike however, you can take the Photography Tour on your last day in the island. This is something you definitely don't want to miss because the Photography Tour will give you as much Instagram-upload material as possible. The beauty here is that you'll be with a guide who knows exactly where and how to take your picture so you'll get the best angle in any given image. Memories are great – but fantastic pictures of you will make sure those memories are as amazing as possible.

SANTORINI - GREECE 🇬🇷

28

Conclusion

Santorini, Greece is a once in a lifetime vacation experience that deserves a spot in your Bucket List. While there's every chance that you'll visit it again, it makes sense to check out all the prime spots of the islands – just in case you have a hard time scheduling a second visit.

Keep in mind that your itinerary depends largely on your flight schedule, the time of the month of your visit, and your budget. It makes sense to figure out all of these beforehand, so you'll be able to follow a specific strategy while you're on the island. If prepared, you'll find yourself enjoying the experience more as all the worries melt away during this perfect vacation under the hot Greek sun!

29

MYKONOS INTRODUCTION

This book contains everything you need to know to enjoy your holiday in the island of Mykonos in Greece.

The island is considered a paradise and travel haven, especially by people who love the beach. It is also offers a lot of party venues day and night.

This book provides insights about the place and its culture. This way, you'll know what to expect before booking your tour. It is best that you come to the island prepared since it is considered one of the most expensive islands in Greece.

The trip will all be worth it. Aside from parties and beaches, the place has rich archaeological and historical findings. It's like a painting everywhere you go.

This book gives a detailed guide on the places that you must check out, food to eat, and other itineraries that you should not miss out during your stay.

Here you'll find a list of the top budget hotels, restaurants, bars, cafes, and many more. It also gives essential tips on the other must-haves that you need to bring on your tour to the island.

Thanks for downloading this book, I hope you enjoy it!

30

Brief History and Background

Mykonos, also known as "The Island of the Winds," is one of Europe's top tourist destinations known for parties, beaches, and nightlife. It caters to people who love to party and have a fun and relaxing holiday. The island is also rich in archaeological finds, symbolizing its history and culture.

This Greek island, which is part of Cyclades, can be found in between Naxos, Paros, Syros, and Tinos. Mykonos got its name from a local hero, Mykonos or Mukovoc, who is said to be the grandson or son of the god Apollo.

It has many seasonal streams with no rivers. Two of its streams have been turned into reservoirs. The island is mainly composed of granite and rocky terrains with eroded areas caused by strong winds.

The size of its area is 85.5 square kilometers that house about 10,134 people according to 2011 census. Most of the island's inhabitants live in the Mykonos or Chora, its largest town found on the west coast. According to history, one of the four major tribes of ancient Greece, the Ionians, established this town in the 11th century B.C. They were the second to inhabit the island after the Carians.

Until the latter part of the 1900s, the eastern side of the island was a rich source of barite, a mineral utilized in oil drilling as a lubricant and clay. Since the island lacks bodies of water, its seawater undergoes the reverse osmosis process to meet its inhabitants and visitors' requirements. The process is able to produce 4,500 cubic meters of water every day.

It used to be a poor island due to the lack of agricultural resources and many of its early inhabitants worshipped many gods and became polytheists. Its location made it an important place for transit and supplies, especially since it is about 2 kilometers away from Delos, its neighboring island with a bigger population.

At the time of the Roman Empire, the island was placed under the control of the Romans and was then owned by the Byzantine Empire until the 12th century. On the latter part of the 13th century, in the year 1390, the island was turned over to a direct Venetian rule. In 1718, the last of the Venetians left the region after the Ottomans claimed the castle of Tinos.

The island attracted immigrants from islands nearby and became a popular trading center until the end of the 18th century. The people in the island played an important role in the Greek Revolution against the Ottoman Empire, which happened in 1821. They were led by Manto Mavrogenous, their national heroine, an aristocrat who chose the Greek cause over her family's fortune. The heroine's statue can now be seen at the center of the main town's square.

The island prospered but suffered losses through time, especially after the First World War. It forced a lot of its natives to migrate to other countries, such as the United States, and in mainland Greece. In 1873, work in the neighboring island of Delos began after the French School of Archaeology started important excavation jobs. It led to the dominance of tourism in the island's economy and a long period of prosperity. The island also suffered after a disaster struck Delos but it has already made its mark in tourists, especially those who were part of the high society in many places from around the globe.

Mykonos is now hailed as one of the most popular travel meccas. The residents of the island have done great improvements in order to make up for whatever it is that they are lacking. They devised a great model for topic tourism and offered high-quality services and facilities to meet the demands of all kinds of tourists.

The island is among the most visited in the Aegean, in the same level of Santorini, despite being more expensive than the other islands in Greece. Partying on the island is a lifestyle. It involves late nights and loud music.

If you happen to book a room at the town's center, expect people to be up and about in the wee hours of the morning. They can be local bakers arriving from work or people coming back from partying and clubbing.

Traffic is a common scenario in the main town's streets but locals use motorized vehicles to go about their day undisturbed by closed roads. These vehicles cause noise, which can disturb you if you happen to book in a room without air conditioning. If you plan to open your windows while you sleep, make sure that you put some earplugs to make sure that you'll get a good rest.

Early season from the middle of May to June, is the best time to visit the island when the weather is not that hot and accommodation is cheaper. You can also book during the postseason of September up to the middle part of October. It gets crowded with tourists during the months of July to August.

AEGEAN SEA

MYKONOS - GREECE

Its main communities are **Ano Mera** and its capital and port town, **Chora**. Ano Mera is situated 7 km east of Chora. This small village is the only inland settlement in the island. This is where you'll find its most significant highlight, the monastery of Panagia Tourliani.

Chora is one of the most crowded Aegean towns with picturesque surroundings and architecture. It maintains its identity and character with the Cycladic architectural style despite being crowded with restaurants, bars, cafes, art galleries, boutiques, and little shops. You'll find shops of known brands, such as Louis Vuitton, Burberry, and Chanel, which mostly cater to tourists coming from cruise ships.

There are other small communities on the island, which include the following:

Agios Stefanos. It houses a lot of good cafes, taverns, restaurants, and hotels.

Agios Ioannis. It became popular after it was used as the location for the film, Shirley Valentine. It is a small settlement with one tiny store, one restaurant, and two taverns.

Tourlos. This is used as a docking station of most cruise ships. Fishing boats and private yachts use the marina and the port welcomes other ferries coming from nearby islands and the mainland.

Ornos. Here you'll find a number of good choices where you'll stay, as well as a food market complete with pharmacy, grocery, bakery, and butcher's shop.

Platys Gialos. This is among the most sought after tourist resorts on the island. Tourists can ride small fishing boats to go to the island's southern beaches.

Climate

The climate in the island is characterized by mild winters and hot and dry summers when it hardly ever rains. Expect rain showers from the months of October to April. Meltemi or constant wind makes the heat more bearable during the months of July to August when the temperatures range from 30 degrees Celsius in the day and 22 degrees Celsius at night. The best months to go to enjoy the beaches start from mid-May to mid-October when the sun and warmth are bearable.

Language

Permanent residents of the island speak Greek but can also communicate in English and other foreign languages.

31

Best Time to Go, Weather, and Safety on the island

Mykonos offers both simplicity and glamour. It's the perfect place for people who want to have a good time mixed with tradition and history. It is generally safe to roam the island. You only have to be alert and careful, especially when exploring busy and narrow streets.

Since partying is a norm in the place, it cannot be helped that there are frequent cases of drunk driving. You also have to study the twists and turns of the roads if you want to ride a quad bike or motorbike to avoid mishaps.

Other than that, the island offers an exciting venture worth the money that you'll spend visiting the place. It offers a place to feel free and fabulous, perfect for those who simply want to have fun and forget about their worries while on vacation.

Best Time to Visit

Plan ahead your trip to the island depending on your preference and itineraries.

Late October to April (Low season) – It's the winter season so expect rain, cool weather, and gray skies. There are limited flights and ferry schedules. There'll be at least a ferry going to Syros and Athens per day. Only a few restaurants and hotels are operating, but they are enough since you'll also have limited activities.

May, June, September, and start of October (Shoulder season) – The island experiences sunny weather these months. It will be warm but not as hot as the summer season. The sea may not be suitable for swimming during the months of May and October because the water's warmth may not be enough. There are also certain establishments closed during these two months, unlike in June and September when everything is open. These months are great for those who prefer to visit without a lot of crowds.

July to early September (High season) – Expect lots of people but the island never gets too crowded so you'll still have a pleasant stay. It is sunny and hot, which makes the seawater most ideal for swimming. This is also the season preferred by those who want to experience Mykonos' famed nightlife. There are many scheduled flights and ferries but expect the prices to be at their peak.

Island Travel Guide by Plans

For people who want to enjoy the island on good weather, plan your trip in between the months of June to September when Mykonos and all Greek islands experience the warmest weather.

If you enjoy soaking in seawater, summer season starts in June but most beach bums would love the water temperature during the warmest months in the island from August to early September.

For tourists who want peace but also prefer to visit the island to swim, you can come in May and October. Most visitors who prefer to enjoy the nightlife visit the island during the peak of the summer season.

If you want to have fun and party during your stay, you can experience the famed nightlife on the island from May to early October. The peak of the parties at clubs and beaches happen from the latter part of June to late July or early August.

If you are on a tight budget but would still love to experience a stay on the island, go during the shoulder season in the months of April, May, and October. Hotels are cheaper during these months but the prices of transportation, drink, and food relatively stay the same. To visit on good weather with cheap hotel prices, the best months include the latter part of May, the start of June, and late September. You can also try your luck during the start of October when visitors are often surprised by good weather.

For tourists who want to visit both Mykonos and Santorini, ferries run between the islands from the early part of April until late in October. It is often a small ferry, SeaJet, which travels in the months of April, May, and October. If you aren't fond of bumpy rides, you can travel from June to September when the larger ferry, Hellenic, can bring you to both islands. If you happen to travel from November to March, you can still travel between the islands by fly or ferry via Athens.

If you intend to experience island hopping, some of the islands near Mykonos include Ios, Paros, Naxos, and Santorini. Among these islands, Santorini has the longest tourist season that you can visit from the latter part of April until the start of November. You can explore the other islands from the middle part of May to early October.

Island Travel Guide by Month

March – It's the end of the winter but the weather remains cool. By the end of the month, almost half of the hotels and restaurants will be open.

April – About 75 percent of the business establishments on the island will be open by the end of April. Weather will be warmer, which makes it possible to swim and sunbathe. You'll find a few open bars in Mykonos

Town but the nightlife in the island is still relatively quiet.

May – All restaurants and hotels are open by mid-May. There will be many nightlife activities in Mykonos Town. It's the beginning of summer and the weather is nice. Tourists also start to flock the island.

June – There will be lots of beach parties complete with DJs by the middle of the month. Nightlife on the island is at its peak, all the businesses are open, and the weather is great.

July – You will experience crazy and fun parties at bars in Mykonos Town. This is a great time for beach parties. The weather is hot and it is almost the height of summer.

August – The island experiences beautiful weather and it is the busiest month with crazy nightlife at the beach and in town.

September – The great weather on the island continues. Everything is still open and a lot is going on, but the activities and nightlife begin to get a little quiet. The last grand club party usually happens in the middle of this month.

October – The weather is still great for beaches at the start of the month. Many restaurants and hotels start to close by the middle of October and the island feels quiet by its end.

November – Most beaches are deserted but you may be able to swim if the weather permits at the start of the month. It's almost like winter but you can still catch some goings-on in Mykonos Town.

December to February – It's wintertime when the weather is temperate with chilly winds, grey skies, and plenty of rain.

32

Essential Travel Tips to Mykonos

Typical Costs When Traveling to Mykonos

The prices of shared rooms on Airbnb start at 15 EUR. You can also rent studio apartments or an entire home for 50 EUR/night, same price range as 2-star hotels. These hotels have the basic amenities you'll need, such as free WiFi, air-conditioning, and private bathrooms. The said prices can go higher on peak travel seasons, including summer.

If you're in search of cheap hostels, you can get them on Paradise beach. Prices start at 15 EUR/night. The prices are expected to shoot up during summer.

Expect to spend on food during your visit to Mykonos. A light dinner of pasta and cocktail can cost you around 25 EUR. If you are planning on cooking your own food, allot 55 EUR for your weekly groceries. When dining out on a tight budget, avoid the restaurants in the main town. You can also choose to eat pizza and gyros most of the time to take it easy on your budget.

When it comes to transportation, taking the taxi around the island will cost about 20 EUR per person. It can be difficult to hail one, especially during peak travel seasons. You can take the bus, which frequency depends on the season. Buses typically leave every 30 minutes to 1 hour and tickets cost around 1.60 EUR to 2 EUR. The cheapest way to get around town aside from walking is by renting a moped. It costs 10 EUR per day during the low travel season and 22 EUR during the peak season. It is important to note that you'll be asked for a licensed before you can rent a moped or scooter.

How much do you need every day to survive on the island?

It depends on your preferred accommodation. If you are working on a tight budget, around 60 EUR is enough as long as you'll stay in a hostel, use local transport, and cook your own meals.

Money Saving Tips

If you really want to experience Mykonos but can't afford the high costs the island is known for, the following money saving tips can help in easing your expenses:

1. Look for accommodation out of town. The farther these places are from the main town, the cheaper the cost will be. You can take the bus to explore other places and in going to Mykonos Town.

2. Feed your hunger with street snacks and gyros. You can always allot a certain amount to try the island's special delicacies once or twice during your stay depending on how much money you still have.

3. Travel before the peak travel season, specifically before June.

4. Take the overnight ferries in exploring other nearby islands since they are priced lower. It is also recommended to book your tickets in advance, which can give you up to 25% off from the usual ticket cost.

Travel Essentials when Traveling to Mykonos

Expect the unexpected when in Mykonos. The sun may be hot during the day but the nights can get cool, plus it can be windy any time of the day.

While some place seems quiet and relaxing, other places are loud and crowded.

Here are some travel essentials you need to pack when traveling to this island:

1. Cash

While they accept credit cards in most places on the island, you cannot always be guaranteed unlike when you bring cash. As many tourists say, cash is king in Greece and this also holds true on the island. You'll need a few euros when paying for valet parking at the beaches. You also never know when you spot some items that you'd like to buy and bring home.

2. Mosquito repellent

Not only tourists flock the island during summertime but also mosquitoes and other bugs. The last thing that you would want to mind while on vacation is the insects' pesky and itchy bites. Have the repellant handy day and night.

3. Sunscreen

Bring your own sunscreen to avoid buying one on the island, which could be way more expensive. Make sure that you apply it all over your body before heading out and reapply dutifully. Apply your mosquito repellant as well even though you already have the sunscreen.

4. Sunglasses and hat

You'll find them useful anywhere on the island, especially when you are taking a boat ride. They will make it easier for you to always come prepared for the cameras when a nice view appears on sight.

5. Medicines

Take your own medications, especially when you are taking specific ones for certain illnesses. Aside from being expensive, it may be hard to look for specific medicines once you are on the island. To be sure that you'll enjoy your vacation, pack the following items in your bag: lozenges for sore throats, antihistamines for allergies, itch relief cream for insect bites, Dramamine for sea voyages, Dioralyte for hangovers and dehydration, and paracetamol for headaches.

If you are used in applying gels and creams for body pains, bring them as well. The last thing that you would want to happen while in this beautiful paradise is to get sick or worse, end up in a medical center.

6. Comfortable sandals and shoes

Expect a lot of walking while on the island. Make sure that you're always wearing comfortable footwear to make the most out of the experience. You can also buy locally made sandals and even bring some pairs at home. Flip-flops are not advisable when walking around. They are only fit when you are on the beaches and treading the sand.

7. Toiletries

You have to be always ready to party wherever you are. Bring your toiletries with you so you can freshen up any time that you're feeling the need for a touch-up. Bring your comb, hair accessories and products, make-up and powder, hand sanitizer, perfume, and wipes.

8. Jacket and trousers

The nights can be windy and cool on the island and the weather is generally unpredictable during the day. Make sure that you have something to wear to beat the cold when it strikes.

9. Gadgets and cameras

Make sure that your gadgets have enough memory storage because you will be taking a lot of pictures no matter where you are on the island. Bring your gadgets suitable for dry and wet conditions, as well as the types that you can bring underwater. Pack the batteries and chargers as well to be certain that your cameras or phones are always ready to take the perfect pictures wherever and whenever.

10. Books

Expect some downtime even when you're on a holiday. Use this time to catch up on books that you've always wanted to read but couldn't get enough time to finish.

11. Drivers license

This is necessary if you are planning to rent a car while you are on the island. It can be quite difficult to catch taxis, especially during the peak season.

33

Transportation

When it comes to transportation, your options on how to get to the island vary on the time of your visit.

By Air

Its airport, the Mykonos Island National Airport (JMK IATA), is situated about 4 kilometers away from the town's center.

There are fewer frequent flights from Volos, Crete, Santorini, and Rhodes via Sky Express during high season. You can catch direct flights from Thessaloniki every day via Aegean Airlines and Olympic Air during summer. You can get to the island via Astra Airlines from Thessaloniki during the months of July and August.

There are direct charter airlines that fly to the island from May to October from the following European airports:

Madrid (MAD) and Barcelona (BCN) – Vueling

Bari (BRI), Napoli (NAP), Palermo (PMO), and Venice (VCE) – Volotea

Milan Orio al Serio (BGY) – Trawel Fly

Paris Orly (ORY) and Amsterdam (AMS) – Transavia

Manchester (MAN) and London Gatwick (LGW) – Thomson Airways

Brussels (BRU) – Jetairfly and ThomasCook

Amsterdam (AMS) – TUIfly

Zurich (ZRH) and Geneva (GVA) – Edelweiss Air

Rome Fiumicino (FCO), Paris Orly (ORY), Milan Malpensa (MXP), Geneva

(GVA), and London Gatwick (LGW) – EasyJet

Istanbul Sabiha-Gokcen (SAW) – Borajet

Rome Fiumicino (FCO) – Blue Panorama Airlines

Istanbul Sabiha-Gokcen (SAW) – AtlasGlobal

You'll find offices of the Aegean Airlines, Olympic Air, and the Mykonos Hoteliers Association at the airport. You will also be greeted by a lot of car rental companies, a post box, public phones, cafeterias, shops, and ATM.

You can get a free Mykonos Sky Map, which you can also buy at shops in town, at the airport's luggage collecting hall. At the first floor of the terminal building, departing passengers can drop by at a duty-free shop that sells gift items, travel accessories, cosmetics, perfumes, spirits, and tobacco.

By Boat

There are two ports on the island – the new one in Tourlos and the old port in Mykonos Town. The latter is utilized by the high-speed catamaran services while many ferries use the new port. You have to check the port your boat will use before traveling.

There are high-speed catamaran services and ferries that run daily from Rafina and Piraeus. The cost of the ride depends on the type of ferry. Slower ones cost lower and the faster ones that can take you to your destination half the time cost more than twice.

Most ferries that connect Piraeus in Athens to Mykonos stop operation at the latter part of October. They typically resume services by the month of April. The ride can take you about 3 to 5 hours, depending on what kind of ferry you are riding.

Taking a ferry from Rafina is recommended to people arriving at the Athens' airport. Travel time to Mykonos takes from 2 to 5 hours, depending on the speed of the ferry. Similar to ferries at Piraeus, most of them stop operation at the end of October and gets back to business in April.

You can also take a boat from the other islands in the Cyclades to get to Mykonos. There are less frequent boats going to the island from Anafi, Thirassia, Sikinos, Folegandros, Milos, Kimolos, Sifnos, and Serifos. You can also take the Nissos Mykonos, an overnight ferry that travels every day from Ikaria and Karlovassi and Vathi in Samos.

Daily boat connections can be found in Crete, Santorini, Ios, and Naxos. Boats connecting to Mykonos travel more than once a day from Paros, Tinos, Andros, and Syros.

It is not necessary to pre-book your high-speed or ferry ride, except during the middle part of July until the end of August. If you booked your ticket online, you have to go to a travel agency to collect your ticket once you have arrived in Greece.

Many of the high-speeds and ferries coming from Rafina and Piraeus stop at Tinos. The latter is expected to be filled with orthodox pilgrims August 15th of every year. Search for the dates when the weekend of Pentecost will happen since many Greek tourists flock Mykonos during this holiday. Make sure to buy your tickets ahead of time if your travel date falls on any of these dates.

Ferrry Phone:

(+30) 2810 346185
(+30) 2810 330598

Email: info@ferries.gr

By Cruise Ship

The island is considered a popular stop by a lot of cruise ship tours traveling to Greece. There are some cruise ships that use the old port but majority docks at the new port. If you arrived at the new port in Tourlos, you can ride the cruise shuttle bus, which will drop you off near the northern bus station in Mykonos Town. You can then explore the town by walking. From the port, you can also opt to hail a taxi but it would be hard to get one if you arrived along with lots of crowds.

You won't need to ride a bus and none will be available when you arrived at the old port. From there, the center of the Mykonos Town is within 10-minute walking distance.

It is not necessary to book guided excursions to enjoy Mykonos. You will enjoy exploring different sights and places by walking alone or with companions.

Getting Around

If you aren't fond of walking or you only have limited days to explore the place, your best option would be a rented scooter or moped. They are cheaper than buses and taxis but users are required to have a license before they are allowed to rent.

Phone:+30 2289 028388 (scooter)

34

Hotels

Filoxenia Apartments

Situated in Ornos, it is 2.5 km away from the town and 100 m away from the beach. It looks cozy with a sun terrace and lounge area. It offers airport transportation, dry cleaning, concierge, free high-speed internet and public WiFi, and free parking.

During your stay, take your time in exploring Ornos, a village that looks picturesque and tranquil. You can book each apartment for 4 people. These apartments have a refrigerator and air conditioning in rooms and bigger rooms have kitchenettes. Smoking rooms are also available upon request. From here, you can check out nearby restaurants, such as To Apomero, Aleka's Restaurant, Bowl, and Markos Falafel.

Phone: +30 2289 026726

Petasos Town Hotel

This romantic hotel is situated near popular landmarks in the island, which include Agios Nikolakis Church, Gioras Wood Medieval Myko-nian Bakery, and Rarity Gallery. This non-smoking hotel offers airport transportation, spa, breakfast, free high-speed internet, bar/lounge, shuttle bus service, and babysitting services. The rooms have a refrigerator, air conditioning, and mini bar.

Nearby attractions include Archaeological Site of Delos, Rarity Gallery, Gioras Wood Medieval Mykonian Bakery, and Lola Bar-Café. From here, you can check out nearby restaurants, such as Karavaki Restau-rant, Thioni Restaurant, Popolo, and Krama.

Phone:+30 2289 022608

Amazing View Hotel

This relatively new hotel is located near Chora and Saint Stefanos beach. The atmosphere is romantic from its location to the hotel's design. It is situated on a hilltop overlooking the Aegean Sea. Staying at this hotel will give you a feeling like you are living in a painting.

It offers airport transportation, free high-speed internet, room service, free parking, laundry service, dry cleaning, and concierge. It has nonsmoking and smoking rooms with kitchenette, refrigerator, and air conditioning. Nearby restaurants include Kapari Restaurant, Taverna Petran, Limnios Tavern, and Reeza Restaurant.

Phone:+30 694 245 7008

Aether Boutique Stay

Situated 800 km away from the town, this hotel is near famous attractions, such as Megali Ammos, Mykonia, and The Garden. It is also near the beaches and surrounded by the amazing views of the sea. The architecture is a combination of modern and local style. It offers airport transportation, breakfast, free high-speed internet, free parking, non-smoking rooms, multilingual staff, laundry and babysitting services.

Phone:+30 2289 077303

Angela's Rooms

It's a walking distance from the heart of the town with its location near its edge. This hotel is preferred by those who want to stay somewhere quiet. It has one apartment set in a garden and a group of seven rooms built in Mykonian style. The look is simple yet chic adorned with original artwork and simple standard furniture.

The hotel is 2.5 km away from the airport. It will only take you around 2 minutes of walking to get to the bus stop. Psarrou beach is about 4 km away.

Its amenities include non-smoking rooms, refrigerator and air conditioning in rooms, public WiFi, and free high-speed internet. Nearby restaurants include Thioni Restaurant, Krama, I Scream, and Cosmo Café. Aside from beaches, other attractions located near the hotel include Megali Ammos, The Garden, and Gioras Wood Medieval Mykonian Bakery.

Phone: +30 2289 022055

35

Restaurants

You'll never run out of places to eat all over the island. Here are among the top restaurants that offer different specialties and cuisines:

Avli Tou Thodori

This restaurant located at Platys Gialos Beach serves breakfast to late night snacks. They are known for Greek, European, and Mediterranean cuisines. They offer special diets, such as gluten-free, vegan, and vegetarian-friendly.

The restaurant accepts customers by reservations. It has a full bar and serves alcohol. It accepts credit cards and has free WiFi. It is a family business that dates back in the 1960s. Aside from the superb dining experience, it is known for the nice view of the beach and excellent service.

Phone:+30 2289 078100

Indian Palace

This is the place to go if you fancy Indian and Asian dishes. Located in Mykonos Town near Cavo Paradiso, this resto serves meals from lunch to late night dishes and snacks. It caters to special diets, such as gluten-free, halal, vegan, and vegan-friendly. It has an extensive list of wine and offers Indian lager beer. The place has a great view of the sea and your dining experience will be accompanied by Indian music. It has a hall that can accommodate 150 guests and a separate hall for business meetings and parties fit for 100 people.

Phone:+30 2289 078044

Compass

This relatively new resto-bar is located at Tourlos. It serves Mediterranean and Greek cuisines open from lunch to dinner. It also serves special diets, such as vegan and vegetarian-friendly. It has a superb location overlooking Delos and a great view of the sunset.

Phone:+30 2289 077040

Phos Restaurant

Situated at Platys Gialos inside the Nissaki boutique hotel, this restaurant serves Mediterranean, European, seafood, Greek, and international cuisines. It offers the finest selection of Greek wines. It serves breakfast to dinner and special diets, such as gluten-free, vegan, and vegetarian-friendly. It's the best place to have cocktails while enjoying its view of Psarou beach.

Phone:+30 2289 027666

Kikis Tavern

You'll find this at Agios Sostis beach. It's open from lunch until late at night. It offers barbecue, Greek, Mediterranean, and seafood cuisines. It serves special diets, such as gluten-free, vegan, and vegetarian-friendly.

Phone:+33 (0)450 230790

36

Best Bars And Night Clubs

Top 5 Bars

The island is brimming with bars where you can enjoy great cocktails, food, and party venues. Here are some of the top choices that you can check out during your stay:

Tropicana Beach Bar & Restaurant

The place is open day and night and is said to be one of the reasons why tourists flock at Paradise Beach where this can be found. It offers breakfast and coffee during the day, tasty dishes at lunch, and loads of food and refreshing cocktails in its all-day beach party, complete with a refined set of DJs. It attracts young and beautiful crowd donning their sexy swimwear, fitting its the Sexiest Beach Bar award given by the Travel
   Channel in 2012.

Phone: +30 2289 023582

Jackie O'

This bar offers fashioned-theme parties held weekly, complete with guest DJs and resident artists. This bar is found at Mykonos Town overlooking the Super Paradise Beach. It's not exclusive to party people but also those who want to lounge at the Jacuzzi or pool or enjoy the view and its famous sunset-watching spot.

Phone:+30 2289 077298

Queen of Mykonos

This posh cocktail bar found at Mykonos Town is a favorite among the young and the beautiful. Most of its guests stay in the place to have a warmup before hitting other party clubs around town. It features DJs later in the evening and known for serving signature cocktails, especially champagne.

Phone:+30 694 661 8539

Void

This sleek bar has only begun its operation in 2017 but has been getting a lot of rave reviews. Located at Mykonos Town, it features DJ talents, including Seth Troxler, Jackmaster, and Damian Lazarus, playing mostly techno beats and deep house. The place has three levels. The void refers to its atmospheric lighting installation, which gives its ceiling the illusion of the night sky. It has a spacious dance area, curvy finishing, and two bars.

Phone:+30 694 481 1360

Kalua Beach Bar

This bar has the reputation of giving out the best beach party on the island. Located on Paraga Beach, this bar, which has been operating for 14 years, lives up to its motto – Every day is a beach party! It caters mostly to the energetic and young crowd who love partying until sunrise. It's open in the day where its highly trained bartenders serve the signature Kalua Watermelon cocktails to beachgoers.

Phone: +30 2289 023397

Top 5 Night Clubs

Mykonos island wouldn't be known as the Ibiza of Greece for nothing. Aside from adoring villages and beautiful beaches, it boasts off great beach parties and dynamic nightlife. Here are the best nightclubs where you can party hard and have fun all night.

Babylon

Babylon is situated near the Panagia Paraportiani church.Located in a seaside matched with nice décor, the club makes a great place to hang out. It plays a variety of music, from oldies, mainstream to techno. The place also holds regular themed parties.

Phone:+30 2289 025152

Cavo Paradiso

This contemporary open-air club is among the most famous on the island. It can be found on Paradise Beach. The club is considered a major player when it comes to parties and nightlife. Thousands of tourists flock the bar every summer. It also invites popular EDM DJs each year. The bar can get too crowded, especially during peak season, so it is recommended to book your table in advance to get the best seats.

Phone:+30 2289 027205

Skandinavian Bar and Club

Situated at the heart of Mykonos Town, this club is a known meeting point on the island. It offers the best cocktails and has an inviting atmosphere to groove the night away. You can choose to have fun at its open-air dance floor or have a good conversation with the more relaxing atmosphere at its patio area.

Phone:+30 2289 022669

@54

@54 is a relatively new dance club on the island.It's the perfect place to mingle around while dancing or sipping champagne. It has a trendy and modern interior with a terrace where you can wait for the sun to set to take your pictures.

Phone: +30 2289 028543

Super Paradise Beach Club

This is considered a party institution inside a private beach, the Super Paradise. This is perfect for hardcore clubbers and it also attracts prominent personalities, including models and celebrities. Music starts in the afternoon but parties can erupt any time. This club features nightly DJ sets. It has a mellow atmosphere during the day suitable for sunbathing or enjoying a drink while strolling or simply enjoying the view.

Phone:+30 698 591 9002

37

Best Cafes or Coffee Shops

Cosmo Cafe

This coffee shop in Mykonos Town is not only a café but also serves Greek cuisines. It also serves special diets, including gluten-free, vegan, and vegetarian-friendly. It is open from breakfast until lunch. It is known for its fast service and good frappe.

Phone:+30 2289 022215

Popolo

Located at Mykonos Town, this café serves breakfast to dinner. It's not only a café but also offers international, Greek, Mediterranean, and Italian cuisines, as well as fast food. It caters to special diets, such as gluten-free, vegan, and vegetarian. It also serves alcohol and offers free Wifi, outdoor seating, table service, and food takeout. It has multilingual staff and home delivery service is available within the city.

Phone: +30 2289 022208

Bowl

Located in Ornos, a lot of people take the trip from the town to this café to taste its wide-range of dishes and drinks while enjoying the laid back atmosphere of the place. Aside from coffee drinks and other beverages, it also serves international cuisines. You can request for special diets, such as gluten-free, vegan, and vegan-friendly. It's actually known for its Vegan Brekkie Bowl, which will be enjoyed even by those who are not on a vegan diet. Most dishes in its menu is served in bowls, hence its name.

Phone: +30 2289 077659

Lalala

This café bar in Mykonos Town serves breakfast, lunch, and drinks. It serves various cuisines, such as European, fusion, and Greek. It also has a wine bar and caters to vegan diets upon request. Clients rave about its coffees and other meals. It is also known for its welcoming and warm staff.

Phone:+30 2289 079305

Cafe Yialos

This café in Mykonos Town serves breakfast to dinner. Aside from coffee and drinks, it also offers Greek and Mediterranean cuisines. It caters to special diets, such as vegan and vegetarian-friendly. The place has a nice view of the seafront and everything on its menu is delicious. The place is simple and food is cooked in a tiny kitchen. It's a good venue to enjoy meals and drinks while chatting with your companions or simply enjoying the view and atmosphere.

Phone: +30 2289 023552

38

Best Famous Landmarks in the Island

You'll never run out of places to go on the island no matter what you'd like to do – beaches, nightlife, shopping, or simply have your pictures taken at scenic sights. Here are three top 5 famous landmarks that many tourists rave about when in Mykonos:

1. Windmills (Kato Myloi)

The windmills are considered iconic in the island and one of its most picturesque landmarks. They are situated on a hill overlooking the Aegean Sea and Mykonos Town. It is a must for every tourist to have their picture taken at this spot.

You'll actually get a glimpse of the windmills upon arriving at the port. These windmills can also be seen at every point of the town so you won't miss them while strolling or roaming around.

There are 16 wheat mills, most of which were built in the 16th century by the Venetians. They used to provide a good source of income for the residents by milling wheat until they ceased to operate in the mid 20th century. The importance of wheat for the island's inhabitants is commemorated to this day in one of the mills' museum.

2. Little Venice

This little neighborhood at the edge of the Aegean Sea is both scenic and romantic. It has an overlooking of the windmills and sea. The spot is considered one of the most beautiful spots in Mykonos Town.

Aside from taking pictures and enjoying the view, it houses lots of restaurants and café bars open day and night during the peak season. You can enjoy food, coffee, and drinks while waiting for the sun to set or filling your cameras with mementos of your trip.

3. Ftelia Archaeological Site

This archaeological site is a must-see for history lovers. Situated at the northern part of the island, the area is filled with a rich history dating back the Neolithic period. According to many, here lays the tomb of Ajax the Locrian, an ancient Iliad war hero. Its excavations revealed a lot of interesting pieces of history during the Neolithic period, such as arrowheads made from obsidian, animal bodies, and fragments of ceramic vessels.

4. Church Of Panagia Paraportiani

This edifice is special and is said to be the oldest church on the island. It is a single structure composed of different architectural styles with five churches built in the 15th to the 17th century. Located between the port and Little Venice, its whitewashed monument looks spectacular from every angle and on any weather.

5. Armenistis Lighthouse

The road going up this lighthouse may be difficult but the effort and travel on the way up are priceless and worth it. You'll find this old lighthouse at the northern part of Mykonos. Its 19-meter towering height will give you a better peek at the panoramic views of the island. Tourists usually come here to enjoy a romantic sundowner picnic or take pictures of the scenery. Make sure that you dress appropriately since it is often windy in this historic lighthouse.

39

Best Museums And Art Galleries

Best Museums

Archaeological Museum

This Archaeological Museum is a small museum found in Mykonos Town and has an excellent location by the beach. You will be delighted at its display of jewelry pieces starting from the Neolithic Period.

Phone: +30 2289 022325

Folklore Museum

Situated next to the Paraportiani Orthodox Church at Mykonos Town, this small museum has some of the most interesting finds. It has a wide array of traditional items that will make you understand more about

Cycladic life. It provides a great history and interesting anecdotes about the island.

Phone: +30 2289 022591

Aegean Maritime Museum

True to its name, this small museum in Mykonos Town displays a wide array of ship models and other objects related to maritime. You'll enjoy bidding your time in this place, especially if this is your interest. The admission to this museum is free. It has a small garden and an old lighthouse where you can take your pictures after the tour.

Phone: +30 2289 022700

Lena's House

This small museum found in Mykonos Town is free of charge but only asks for a donation. It has an interesting display of the costumes and houses typical of the 19th century.

Phone: +30 2289 022390

Agricultural Museum and Boni Windmill

This is another interesting museum in Mykonos Town. You will need to trek uphill to reach the place. The effort will be rewarded with interesting displays of local history and a great view of the town and the windmill where you can take your pictures.

Best Art Galleries

Minima Gallery

The gallery is situated in a lovely small house at Goumenio Square. It features works from Greek artists and other foreign artists, including those from New Zealand, Germany, and Austria. The painting displays are comprehensive and it also has some displays of great sculptures. The decors are minimal, true to its name, so the highlight would be on the artworks.

Phone: +30 2289 023236

Dio Horia

This art platform and gallery is located in Mykonos Town. The gallery stimulates knowledge, creativity, experimentation, and debate with its audience. Aside from the displays of culture and contemporary art, it also presents exhibitions, pop-up bookshops, publications, events, and residencies.

+30 694 472 3636

Eden Fine Art Gallery

This boutique gallery is an International gallery of Pop and Contemporary Art. It has an extensive collection of over 26 contemporary artists from the different parts of the globe. The artworks are evocative, inspiring, and colorful. This well-established gallery has staff knowledgeable about the arts. It looks vibrant and has the perfect location in the beach towns of Psarou.

Phone: +44 7442 553055

The Big White Gallery

Set in an impressive building, the gallery is situated in Mykonos Town. It looks relatively new and has a fine display of both traditional and contemporary artworks. The place is spacious, giving you enough space to observe and appreciate the sculptures and painting inside.

Phone:+44 6945905267

Municipal Art Gallery

It presents a wide range of artworks and art collections. Check its schedule to visit the place in time for its events.

40

List of Special Things You Can Only Do in Mykonos

Discover the reasons why Mykonos is among the most popular islands in Greece. Aside from a great nightlife, it offers a whole lot of activities for families, couples, solo travelers, and gay individuals. It boasts off a friendly and fun atmosphere with special places where you can seek peace and relaxation.

Here are the special and unique things that you must try during your stay in this popular island:

Visit the Mykonos Vioma Organic Farm

The place offers wine tasting while indulging on the island's popular food products, such as Greek salad, loutza or ham, rusks, and cheeses. The farm is located in a peaceful area in the countryside of the island and it is surrounded by farm animals and vineyards. It produces its own honey and organic wine.

Phone: +30 2289 071883

Go on a bicycle tour

You can choose the track and places to go when on a bike tour depending on your ability as a rider. You'll be given safety equipment and proper orientation before starting. This is a great way to visit a lot of sites in a day. Your guide will also explain the sights and give you time to take pictures and souvenirs. You will also be allowed to relax and eat the best delicacies in the island as the tour continues. More advanced riders can opt to continue the tour at neighboring beaches.

Phone: +30 22890 71883 (Yummy Pedals)
   email: yourguide@yummypedals.gr

Walk around the old port

The Pelican, which is a must-see in the island, can be seen at the old port. From this point, you can also opt to visit the neighboring island of Delos via ferry. The old port is home to many restaurants and cafes overlooking the sea. It also offers a picturesque view, great for strolling day and night.

Enjoy signature dishes and cuisine

The island offers hearty dishes with its diverse culinary landscape. Make sure that you try traditional Mykonian dishes during your stay.

Here are some of your best options when it comes to the food that you must try:

Snacks (Meze)

Rafiolia – Fried dough with tirovolia filling and sprinkled with honey, sugar, and cinnamon.

Louza – A dish made from locally grown peppery pork, thinly sliced, and cooked until sweet-scented.

Tirovolia – A mild, fresh cheese popular in the island.

Mostra – This dish is made with olives, barley rusks, sun-dried tomatoes, and kopanisti, sprinkled with oregano, extra virgin olive oil, and capers if preferred.

Noumboulo – This is popular not only in Mykonos but in other Greek islands as well. The dish is smoked pork fillet that does not only smells good but also tastes great.

Ksinotiti – It's a sour cheese, which is a favorite appetizer among locals.

Kopanisti – A slightly spicy cheese with unique aroma.

Seafood

Aside from the beaches popular for recreation, Mykonos is also rich with different varieties of seafood that local fishermen earn from.

Many tavernas and local restaurant serve small fish, such as smelt, sardine, and anchovies along with larger fish, such as seabream and parrotfish. They are typically fried and seasoned with locally produced olive oil. These dishes are best served along with an appetizer, called tzatziki, made from dill, olive oil, vinegar, cucumber, onion, and yogurt.

You can also request for sautéed or fried shrimps and stewed or grilled octopus, both served in a skillet along with olives, feta cheese, and tomatoes.

Great Bakery Finds

Mykonos is a goldmine of breads and other baked treats. Among the favorites include amygdalota or baked cookies made of crushed almonds and tsimbita or little bites with flavors that include honey, cinnamon, and orange. You can also find a famous Greek dessert in the island, baklava, if you are into sweets. It is made of pastry, honey, and chopped nuts.

The island boasts its signature pies, such as honey pie and onion pie and other freshly baked breads. You must also try paximadia or double-baked bread or rusks and kouloures or sesame rings.

To complete the experience, eat these treats along with almond-flavored non-alcoholic beverage, rosewater or soumada.

What to Eat at Tavernas

Taverna is a small restaurant in Greece that serves traditional dishes. You will find a lot of tavernas in Mykonos island. It is the perfect place to eat and have a good time. Aside from food, local wines, and other beverages, the place also involves dancing and entertainment.

These restos serve classic Greek cuisines, such as souvlaki or grilled vegetables or meat on a skewer, gyros or spit-roasted vegetables or meat placed in a pita bread and seasoned with tzatziki, pastitsio or moussaka variation with pasta instead of potatoes and eggplant, and moussaka or baked dish made of minced meat, potatoes, and eggplant and served with béchamel sauce.

The other food that you must try at tavernas includes broad beans with lard and fennel, fried wild mushrooms, snails with onions and pilaf, oporichia with broad beans, cabbage served with lard, fresh amaranth, and fennel fritters with wild fricasseed.

Find out why this island is among the best shopping places in Greece

Many people tag the island as a shopping paradise. All you have to do is to get lost in its town and you'll be thrilled with the variety of merchandise you can get from the tons of shops you'll surprisingly find even at the most unexpected corners.

It is easy to get lost in the cobblestone paved streets of the town. Actually, the streets were built like a labyrinth. This structure was done in purpose as the defense of its inhabitants against the pirates after the Byzantine period. At the time, invaders would enter the town from the port but would get lost in the maze-like design of the streets.

Unlike during the old times, getting lost in the town's streets nowadays entails adventure and fun. You won't get much help from road signs since there are only a few but you can always ask around for a little help when it comes to directions.

If you want to bring home interesting finds from the island, here's the list of the best Mykonos souvenirs:

Hand-woven scarves

The right kind of scarf can make a whole lot of difference in any outfit that you are wearing. It is a fashion must-have when on the island. You can wear it like a shawl or wrap it around your head to get good pictures despite the windy atmosphere. You will find a great selection of scarves at many shops on the island, but the Salt Boutique offers an extensive selection that will fit any kind of look or outfit you're sporting.

Crocheted handbag

The bag is a versatile item that can match your outfit. It is also something that will always remind you of the island and all the fond memories you had during your stay. If you have the budget, you might as well head on to Mykonos Aesthet flagship store found at the Nammos village. You'll find a great selection of crocheted handbags made by local designers, including lines from One & Only. These bags are available in all shapes, sizes, and styles. They can go well in casual or formal wear.

Aesthet Phone:+30 22890 27132

Rugs

Aside from the attractions, the island has an artistic overall appeal. The surroundings are picturesque and all establishments and villages have unique and interesting appeal. Hand-knitted rugs are among the favorites when it comes to souvenirs. It's like bringing a piece of the artistic island into your home. Aside from a variety of designs, you are rest assured that these rugs were made to last. You will find them in many shops, especially at the home accessory shops you'll find along the Chora's Matoyianni Street.

Locally made sandals

They are practical and versatile. They are available in various designs catering to the styles of both males and females. While in Mykonos, make sure that you get them at the shop, which has been around since 1948, the Mykonos Sandals. You'll find it at the Little Venice district near the Veranda Bar. It offers various styles of handmade sandals, from traditional, artistic to contemporary. It wouldn't be hard to find the right design that will fit your personality and style.

Bakery items

Aside from the restaurants, bars, and cafes, you'll find bakeries on the island where you can buy sumptuous items that you can bring home. One of the most famous stores known for its heavenly cakes and pastries is the Gioras Wood Medieval Mykonian Bakery. While you're there, make sure that you try its version of the traditional Greek sweet pastry, known as baklava. The store sells a wide range of bakery goods, such as quiches, buns, cookies, croissants, pies, and unique breads.

Phone:+30 2289 027784

Jewelry

Greek jewelry is well-known all over the world as one of the finest. You will also find local jewelry shops in Mykonos with great choices of carefully crafted and high-quality accessories. If you are serious about buying good jewelry find, check out the Ilias Lalaounis Jewellery, which products were produced at its workshop in Athens.

Phone: +30 2289 022444

Venture into Nudist-Friendly Beaches

It is not uncommon in Greece to find beaches where people prefer to go without anything on. The beauty of the beaches makes it easier even for first timers to take it all off while enjoying the water and nature.

Mykonos continues to be a favorite among who love going to the beaches without bathing suit even though there are no official nude beaches in the place. It was once considered a nudist paradise but now, you can still spot secluded areas and beaches without hoards of crowds.

If you are ready for the adventure, you may want to head on to the following nudist-friendly beaches in Mykonos: Kapari Beach, Agios Sostis Beach, Panormos Beach, Paraga Beach, Agrari Beach, and Elia

Beach.

41

3-day travel itinerary

Mykonos is not exclusive for people who love to party. If you only have three days to explore the island, make sure that you enjoy all the best that it has to offer. It is a small island so you will surely have enough time to accomplish this 3-day travel itinerary.

Day 1: Get acquainted with the island's culture and rich history

While in Mykonos, you can book a boat excursion en route to its neighboring island of Delos. It is known as one of the most important archaeological sites in Greece and considered as a UNESCO World Heritage Site. Take the old port in Mykonos, where daily boat tours going to Delos are available, except on Mondays. Start the tour in the morning since the archaeological site in the island closes at 3 PM. Aside from a breathtaking view, the site is rich in history and is said to be the birthplace of Artemis and Apollo according to mythology.

After the tour in Delos, you can check the romantic and artistic site of Little Venice. Here you can enjoy good food and cocktails while waiting for the sun to set.

Phone:+30 6945123044 (Catamaran)

You can also opt to see the Archaeological Museum of Mykonos in the Old Town before or after going to Little Venice. If you happen to be on the island during the summer months, you can choose to come to the museum at night since it is open until 10 PM. This edifice houses different finds from the island, including funerary urns and stelae, grave statues, and vases of all sizes that date back from the prehistoric era up to the latter part of the Hellenistic period.

Day 2: It's time to party and hit the beaches

The island is famous for its beaches with crystal clear water and golden sand. These beaches have different characters that appeal to the varying tastes of the tourists coming in. Since you can tour all the beaches on the island given the limited days of your tour, choose the ones that fit your personality and style. Here are your best choices when it comes to the best beaches in Mykonos:

Fokos Beach

This secluded beach, situated in the northern part of the island, is only accessible by car. It is preferred by people who want privacy and peace. This beach is popular among nature lovers with its breathtaking natural beauty. The water is not suitable for swimming since the sea can get choppy, especially when it is too windy. It is also a sandy area but the place is unspoiled and the atmosphere is calm. Aside from nature tripping and relaxing, you can also enjoy a wide range of delicious meals in the tavern found in one area of this beach.

Paraga Beach

Its location allows you to experience the best of both worlds. It is comprised of two sandy beachy divided by a headland. If you'll be coming from Platys Gialos, you can choose to walk to reach the beach, which will take about 15 minutes or hop on a bus. The northern side of the beach is great for snorkeling, swimming, and other watersports. It is more organized with music and tavernas. The southern part is more relaxing is peaceful. Overall, the beach offers a fun atmosphere and it is not unusual to go nude while in the place.

Psarou Beach

It is idyllic and picturesque, but this beach situated in the southern part of the island can be expensive and crowded. This is where the popular Nammos beach bar can be found. The beach offers music, bars, many options for restaurants and party venues. It is also known for its turquoise water perfect for scuba diving and snorkeling, golden sands, and a stunning bay.

Platys Gialos

This is a good family beach, accessible by local bus or taxi boat. It is well-organized with many cafes, restaurants, and hotels nearby. The beach has calm water suited for watersports and swimming. It has a long stretch of sand and a lot of sunbed umbrellas, where you can lounge while enjoying a drink or trying to relax.

Elia Beach

This is one of the longest beaches on the island, situated 11 km from Mykonos Town. It is family friendly and has a lot of beach bars, umbrellas, sunbeds, and other facilities. It is frequented by those who love watersports, such as windsurfing, parasailing, and skiing. This popular beach is quieter than the other frequented beaches in Mykonos since this is the last stop of a taxi boat. You will enjoy the beach if you love nature. You can try walking into the hills to get an overlooking of the little bay. You can also seek peace and privacy in a secluded spot in one of its alcoves.

Lia Beach

This is another beach preferred by those who want a peaceful and relaxing atmosphere. This sandy beach is surrounded by hills and known for its crystal blue water. There are rocks at its offshore, which makes the beach suitable for snorkeling and diving. It is perfect for swimming and looks inviting to the whole family. The beach is near Kalafatis and is accessible by taxi or boat. It houses two restaurants known from a wide range of food and drinks, as well as friendly staff.

Super Paradise Beach

If you visit Mykonos during the peak season, make sure that you go to this beach in the morning. Tagged as one of the most popular beaches in Greece, party crowds tend to flock the place, especially at nighttime. It has a splendid blue-green sea and soft, golden sand.

Paradise Beach

This is another nudist friendly beach on the island, situated 6 km from Mykonos Town. It has crystal clear water perfect for swimming and watersports. It also houses plenty of clubs and bars that offer party venues from day till night.

Ornos Beach

The beach can be found 3 km from Mykonos Town. It is accessible by boat or bus. It offers a relaxing place that the whole family will appreciate. It can get crowded at night so if you will come with your kids, it is recommended to enjoy the place during the day. It has clear blue water and soft sands. The beach offers many options for restaurants, cafes, umbrellas, and cafes.

Nightlife

Experience what the island is best known for – nightlife. If you want a relaxing night, you can stroll in the old harbor or watch the sunset at Little Venice. You can also visit restaurants and cafes overlooking the sea. The options are endless when it comes to night parties, such as the Cavo Paradiso, Jackie O, and Scandinavian bar, or its popular beach bars, such as Scorpios and Nammos.

Day 3: Take pictures and buy souvenirs

Windmills

Take your last day on the island slow and relaxing. Start your day by visiting its famous windmills to take pictures and enjoy the view.

Churches

The island has an abundance of churches scattered all over. Never miss out on some of its most popular churches, which include Agios Nikolaos and Panagia Paraportiani.

Shopping

You will find a lot of traditional shops, art galleries, leather goods and jewelry shops, and designer label stores in Mykonos town. As you stroll through the shops, you can take more pictures and enjoy the view of bougainvillea-filled balconies of the town's whitewashed houses with blue windows and doors.

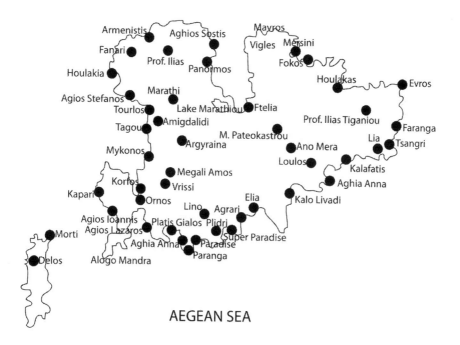

AEGEAN SEA

MYKONOS - GREECE

42

Conclusion

I'd like to thank you and congratulate you for transiting my lines from start to finish.

I hope this book was able to help you to get to know more about the beautiful paradise in Greece, known as the Mykonos Island. I hope that you found insightful ideas that you can use when you head on to the place.

The next step is to plan your trip. Make sure that you pack your things and bring all the necessary items to enjoy your stay on the island.

I wish you the best of luck!

Thank you

I want to thank you for reading this book! I sincerely hope that you received value from it!

If you received value from this book, I want to ask you for a favour .Would you be kind enough to leave a review for this book on Amazon?

Contact- **Gary Jones**: 1highvaluebooks@gmail.com

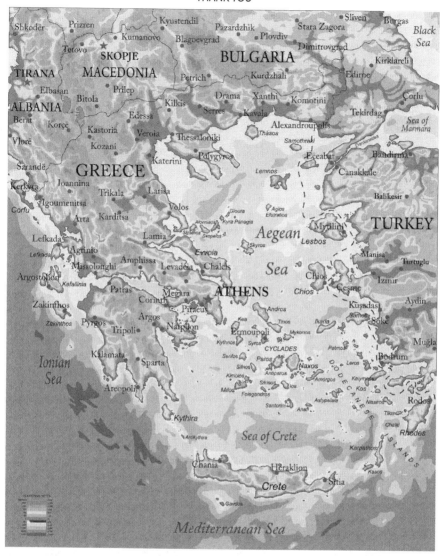

Made in the USA
Columbia, SC
13 April 2021

36002602R00164